Parenting in Perspective

Timeless Wisdom, Modern Applications

MAGGID

Barry Kislowicz

PARENTING IN PERSPECTIVE

Timeless Wisdom, Modern Applications

Maggid Books

Parenting in Perspective
Timeless Wisdom, Modern Applications

First Edition, 2016

Maggid Books
An imprint of Koren Publishers Jerusalem Ltd.

POB 8531, New Milford, CT 06776-8531, USA
& POB 4044, Jerusalem 9104001, Israel
www.korenpub.com

Cover design: Tani Bayer

Cover illustration © Rinat Gilboa

The publication of this book was made possible
through the generous support of *Torah Education in Israel.*

ISBN 978-159-264-456-8, *hardcover*

A CIP catalogue record for this title is
available from the British Library

Printed and bound in the United States

In loving memory of Irving and Beatrice Stone,
who dedicated their lives towards the
advancement of Jewish education.
We are proud and honored to continue in their legacy.

Their Children, Grandchildren, and Great-Grandchildren
Cleveland, Ohio USA

*In sincere appreciation and with
tremendous Hakarat HaTov to
Rabbi Barry Kislowicz
for his leadership and contribution to the
Cleveland Jewish community
and especially to Fuchs Mizrachi School.
We are a better community because of
all that you have given of yourself and we
wish you, Kally and your children
much success and happiness in Israel.
You will be sorely missed.*

*Judy and Morry Weiss
Hildee and Gary Weiss and Family
Karen and Jeff Weiss and Family
Rachel and Zev Weiss and Family
Sara Hurand and Elie Weiss and Family*

Contents

PART II

Preface

In the coming pages, we will share some thought-provoking frameworks for raising and educating our children. Unlike many parenting books, the goal is not merely to equip parents with strategies. Strategies are wonderful, but the crux of the matter lies in the perspective we bring to our parenting.

As we will come to see, perspective is the lens that orients us, forms our goals, shapes our interactions, and directs our parenting efforts. In our case, this lens is founded on Torah values and applied to modern family relationships through the wisdom and insight of current psychological, social, and educational research.

As you read this book, you will come to know two families, the Stein family and the Abram family, whose relationships and approaches to parenting will illustrate, respectively, the perspective we are trying to move beyond and the perspective we hope to embrace. If you are like most of us, you may find yourself wondering, "I snapped at my kids yesterday...but I also spent some good quality time with them. Am I a Stein or an Abram?"

Of course the truth is that each of us is a mix of the two. Our goal in presenting the Abram family is simply to illustrate what our perspective looks like in practice. This illustration inspires us to reflect on our parenting as we stretch ourselves to apply these concepts to our own lives. We may not fully live up to the example set by our fictional Abram family, but we, and our children, will be better off for the effort.

ACKNOWLEDGEMENTS

This project began with a chance conversation around a Shabbat table. I am deeply indebted to Mr. Morry Weiss for sparking that discussion, based on his conviction that more Modern Orthodox ideas need to be brought to the community. Beginning with that discussion, Morry and the entire Weiss family have been a major source of leadership, encouragement, and support in bringing the book to fruition. In particular, I must also thank Zev Weiss for his time in reading each chapter as it was produced and sharing his honest feedback.

For the last twelve years, I have been privileged to be a part of the Fuchs Mizrachi School community in Cleveland, Ohio. Many of the insights and practical foundations for this work flowed from my invaluable experience at Mizrachi. I must single out the members of the Mizrachi community with whom I have had the honor of working most closely over the years: my colleagues on the lay and professional leadership teams, my executive coach, and the inspirational educators who have always pushed me to do more. Throughout my time here, I have been inspired by Mizrachi versions of the Abram family. I must note, however, so as to preserve the sanctity of these relationships, that none of the anecdotes in this book is drawn directly from real life in Cleveland. They are all illustrations of my own creation.

Thanks are also due to Matthew Miller, Rabbi Reuven Ziegler, Tomi Mager, and the staff of Maggid Books for seeing the project to fruition, and to Robert Milch and Shoshana Rotem for skillfully proofreading the text.

Writing this book has deepened my understanding of the complexity and challenge inherent in parenting. It has also reinforced my appreciation for my own parents, who taught me by example what it means to treat children as independent individuals and to support them as they grow along their own paths. Of course, in my case this included their reading drafts of this book and providing helpful feedback and encouragement.

My extended family, in-laws, and siblings have likewise been role models for developing committed, loving relationships in every respect. These relationships have both supported and inspired me throughout my life, and this project is no exception.

Closest to home and closest to my heart, I must thank my immediate family. My children, Matan, Yair, Aviad, and Shefa, who have made my task as a parent so blessed. One piece of advice that I did not include in this book: The easiest way to be a good parent is to start out with great kids. Finally, my wife Kally, who edited every sentence of this work (other than this one), and whose encouragement to take life one day at a time, to stay balanced, and to remember to enjoy things along the way not only enabled me to complete this project but, more important, is the key to our beautiful family, all that we accomplish together, and the life for which I thank God every day.

Introduction

How Did That Happen?

THE ABRAM FAMILY

There is one in every community. That family you see in the hallways at school or on the checkout line at the supermarket. We will call ours the Abram family.

David Abram is a successful lawyer who is a partner in a small firm in town. Sara Abram is an occupational therapist working at a senior-living facility. They have both volunteered at the shul and JCC, and Mr. Abram is currently the school board's treasurer. All in all, they are similar to most of the families in your community. Yet somehow, while most of us are struggling with our kids, they turn out child after child who is the envy of the community. It's not that Ben, Jonny, and Lisa are brilliant, or that they are the stars of every varsity team. It's that everyone knows the Abram kids are *good kids*. They are the kids who will say good morning to you or offer to help you with whatever you are doing. They are the kids who enjoy sitting next to their parents in shul. They are the kids who seem to have forgotten about the teenage rebellion stage that your kids are putting you through right now.

Mr. Smithson, the school maintenance man, pulled Mrs. Abram aside at pickup time one afternoon to talk about her middle school son. Mr. Smithson does not typically conduct parent-teacher conferences, so the meeting caused a few inquisitive heads to turn. The story? Earlier that day, a middle school student had spilled his bag of chips in the hallway. Like any good middle schooler, he kept right on walking. The students he was with kept walking too. Except one. Jonny Abram stopped in the middle of the hallway to pick up the chips. He was still there when maintenance arrived to sweep up the spill, and Jonny kept right on helping. The parents who had turned to listen went back to their pickup routines. While the event was notable to Mr. Smithson, everyone else had come to expect such behavior from the Abram kids.

One kid like this could be an accident, but three in a row is a pattern. No one is quite sure how the Abrams do it. Especially that other family down the road. We'll call them the Steins. Dan Stein owns a growing medical practice in town. He is deeply involved in the community and is the president of the local shul. Debbie Stein is an associate at a marketing firm who also volunteers as the day school's communications director. The Steins are a typical family in the community, and their children are somewhat typical as well.

THE STEIN FAMILY

Dr. Stein is at shul on time every Shabbat morning. His sixteen-year-old son Adam is sitting right next to him, scowling as he looks down at the closed siddur in his clenched fingers. Rachel, the Stein's twelve-year-old, just had her bat mitzva. She dutifully worked with her tutor to prepare a speech about being kind to others, and she put some effort into the project she had chosen:

knitting scarves to donate to a local men's shelter. When the time finally came to celebrate, Rachel read her speech beautifully, and the guests were quite impressed with her poise and confidence. The Steins wanted to feel only pride in their daughter. They could not help noticing, though, that while Rachel prepared a wonderful bat mitzva speech about kindness, the lesson seemed to have disappeared when it came time to invite *all* the girls in Rachel's sixth-grade class. It took the Steins days of fighting to convince their daughter not to exclude anyone. And once all the girls were at the party, Rachel had found a way to arrange the table so that only her own clique had any chance of talking to her.

Routine twelve-year-old behavior? Absolutely. But the Steins had hoped for so much more from their daughter on her big day. They worried that this was how Rachel now behaved in school all too often. They had already started to receive phone calls from the principal because of how Rachel was treating other girls. The Steins ended the bat mitzva as they ended too many days with their children, wondering if all parents feel quite like this.

HOW DID THAT HAPPEN?

Some families are blessed with child after child who makes them proud. Others seem to struggle with their children at every turn. What separates the Abrams from the Steins? Genetics? Providence? Dumb luck?

Long before a child speaks her first word, her parents are dreaming about her future. They want to protect her and care for her. They want her to be healthy, happy, and successful in her life. As committed Jewish parents, we want all this and more. We want our children to embrace our Torah and embody its values. We want them to be learned, practicing Jews anchored by deep ties to our community and committed to transmitting these values to their own children. We want them to be good, decent people.

Any parents will tell you that they will do whatever it takes to make these dreams come true. Yet in practice, many of us do not know how to help our kids. We work hard to raise and guide our children, but often we find ourselves feeling more like the Steins than the Abrams.

No one has a foolproof recipe for successful parenting. Many factors are beyond our control even in the lives of "normal" kids, to say nothing about children who struggle with physical illness, disabilities, or the like. Yet if we pay close attention, we will notice that families like the Abrams seem to follow a particular pattern in their parenting and family life. The Steins are good people and good parents, but they follow a different set of patterns.

PATTERN AND PERCEPTION

There are no guarantees, but if we can illuminate the key perceptions and practices that make up the Abrams of our world, we can tilt the odds in our favor. As we will see, none of these are quick-fix techniques. Bringing them to bear in our lives can require a fundamental change in how we see our families, our children, and ourselves.

We want our children to adhere to a complex set of values, successfully navigate an array of challenging situations, and emerge with a sense of wholeness and commitment. But we cannot tell our children exactly how to get there. No matter how much guidance we share or how many morality lessons we teach, we will fall short.

And so we must begin by adjusting our perceptions. Our role is not to offer instruction and criticism to the lead actors until they get the scene right. The successful parent is more stagehand than director, understanding that the task is to carefully construct the environments and relationships of which their child is the center. Of course, any loving parents will tell you that their child is the center of their lives. But what does it mean to truly place the child at the center?

Part I

Chapter One

Putting the Child at the Center

Tell the Steins that they do not put their children at the center of their lives and you are not likely to get a kind response. Their anger or incredulity would be quite understandable. Consider for a moment the fortune they spend each year on day school and summer camp, not to mention the clothing, phones, assorted toys, and the recent bat mitzva. Ninety percent of the family budget is spent on the children. The family schedule follows a similar pattern. Carpool runs occupy each morning and afternoon, and Sundays are spent shuttling between soccer games, play practice, and tutoring sessions. Dr. Stein loves taking the kids out to watch the local NBA or MLB teams play, and the whole family vacations together at least once a year.

The Steins will tell you their children are most certainly the center of their lives. And the evidence would seem to support them. If you were to compare their schedule to the Abram family's, you would not find any glaring differences. So what are the Steins missing?

PERCEPTION

The truth is that spending a lot of time or money on something may not be the most meaningful indicator of what is at the "center" of one's life. At least not in a way that is helpful in raising children. Take the middle-aged man down the block who recently purchased a sports car. He has likely spent the majority of this year's salary on the car. He drives the car to work, he drives it around the block, and when he is not driving it, he is washing and waxing it in his driveway. By the barometers of time and money, the car may well be said to be the center of his life.

Putting aside the question of misplaced priorities for a moment, this example illustrates that the investment of time, money, and even energy is not a helpful indicator as we attempt to understand what it means to put our children at the center. Few parents would want to see their efforts at childrearing compared to the obsession of a midlife crisis. Yet if we are not careful, our devotion to our children may have more in common with the sports car than we would care to admit.

What can caring parents possibly have in common with our sports car driver? Perception.

All that we pour into our children will fall flat if we make the mistake of seeing them as passive *objects* at the center of our lives. To place children at the center in a meaningful way, we must view them not as objects in our lives but as the *subjects* of their own.

The driver may care deeply about the sports car, but we would not expect him to think about whether sheltering it in the garage will stunt its long-term development. We certainly would not expect him to allow the car to make its own choices about how fast to drive or what route to take. Yet this is exactly what we must do with our children. We must see them as independent individuals who are the central actors in their own lives. Lives which we are privileged to support, inspire, and sustain as their parents, but lives which, in the final analysis, are fundamentally independent.

ANSWERS

How can we treat our children as independent individuals?

One helpful way to start is by considering how we answer their questions. Especially the tough ones. For example, what did the Steins answer seven years ago when Rachel, then age five, looked up from a puzzle she was working on and asked, "Why is there a moon?"

Debbie Stein took the question very seriously. Thinking back to her own childhood education, she remembered a rabbinic teaching about the first days of Creation. Smiling at her preschooler, she led her over to the living room sofa, where the two sat down together. "Let me tell you a story," she began. "When God created the world, He made two large lights, the sun and the moon. They were both beautiful and equally bright. The sun was quite happy, but the moon became upset. The moon complained to God, 'Both the sun and I can't be the same size. How will people know who is in charge? How will they know which of us is more important?' 'You're right,' responded God, and quickly shrank the moon to a much smaller size because of its jealousy." Debbie finished and looked at Rachel, who seemed to have enjoyed the story and was eager to go back to finishing her puzzle.

Mrs. Stein walked away from this gratifying mother-daughter moment certain that she had just scored an A in parenting. Most of us would feel similarly. Debbie does indeed deserve credit for setting aside time and attention for her daughter, and for sharing a beautiful story from our tradition. Yet there may be another side to this experience. While Debbie had transmitted a teaching, she had also subtly conveyed that she was the source of knowledge, that she had the answers, and that Rachel's job was to sit nicely and listen to her mom's explanations. Mrs. Stein believed she had helped Rachel learn something new, yet in her attempt to teach, she may have actually undercut her child's independence.

QUESTIONS

The Italian educator Carlina Rinaldi suggests a strikingly simple alternative: "When your child asks, 'Why is there a moon?' don't reply with a scientific answer. Ask him, 'What do you think?'"[1] To many of us, this answer sounds like a cop-out, a creative way of avoiding the question if we ourselves do not know the answer. But imagine what would happen if Debbie had taken Rinaldi's approach:

Five-year-old Rachel looked up from her puzzle to ask, "Why is there a moon?" Debbie took the question very seriously. She turned to Rachel and asked, "What do you think?" Rachel kept working on her puzzle, but Mrs. Stein could see the wheels begin to turn. She let Rachel continue to play. A moment later, Rachel looked up and said, "Maybe God did not want us to be scared at night. Just like you put a nightlight in my room." Rachel kept working on the puzzle, rattling off more questions for her mom as she did. Each time Debbie let Rachel make the first suggestion and lead the discussion.

Taking Rinaldi's approach, Mrs. Stein would not have taught her daughter the rabbinic lesson mentioned above. But Rachel would have learned something much more important. She would have learned that her own thoughts mattered, that she was her mother's partner in exploring the world, and that she had a role to play in her own growth process.

---

1. Quoted in Louise Boyd Cadwell, *Bringing Reggio Emilia Home: An Innovative Approach to Early Childhood Education* (New York: Teachers College Press, 1997), 65.

When we respond to our children in this way, we are teaching them a different vital lesson from the story of Creation. The Bible describes human beings as created in the image of God and imbued with the unique capacity for independent thought and free moral choice. When we value our children's thoughts, we teach them that they are fundamentally capable of independent thought and free choice – whether they are five or fifteen – at their own developmental level. More important, we demonstrate to them that we *know* they are capable of independent thought.

To be fair, we must admit that any parent of a five-year-old faces at least a hundred questions a day. It is neither possible nor appropriate to respond like Rinaldi to all of these questions. But those of us who find Rinaldi's approach surprising may want to reexamine *how* we are placing our children at the center of our lives.

We devote an astounding amount of our time, attention, and life's resources to our children, and we deserve credit for doing so. Yet some of us still refer to our children as prized or most precious "possessions," and even those of us who recoil at the phrase may find that it is all too accurate a description of how we see our kids.

DOWN THE LINE

If the questions of a five-year-old do not strike us as particularly difficult, consider how Debbie will respond a few years down the line when teenage Rachel asks why bad things happen to good people, or why God cares what we do or don't do on Shabbat.

Even if Debbie is well equipped to share Judaic or philosophical perspectives on such complex issues, launching into these responses will reveal once again that she sees Rachel as a passive recipient of her adult knowledge, as a dependent object. Anyone who has tried to persuade a teenager to do the day's homework, drive safely, or listen to any form of rule knows exactly how teenage Rachel will respond to her mother's explanations.

On the other hand, if year after year Debbie routinely responds to questions by inviting Rachel herself into the process, demonstrating that Rachel is a full partner in her own growth, she will establish a very different dynamic. Rachel will learn that she plays an active role in making sense of the world. She will be perturbed by the question of why bad things happen to good people, but she will understand that it is her own responsibility to work through this question together with her parents.

For her part, Debbie will not feel the need to answer Rachel's questions. She knows that simply answering the question would be selling her daughter short. Rachel is not a passive vessel to be filled. Rachel is an active participant, an independent partner whose growth and exploration Debbie must support and guide.

BUT WILL HE BE A DOCTOR?

Learning how to respond to our children's questions is a vital ingredient in our attempt to truly place them at the center. But it is far from the only ingredient. In order to treat our children as independent entities, we must examine what lies at the heart of all our parenting decisions.

Consider the following conversation, so typical of what is heard in a principal's office:

> *Dr. Stein:* I wanted to come see you right away. My wife and I are very concerned about our son's grades in AP Biology.
> *Principal:* I certainly understand. I know that Adam's teacher has been concerned as well. AP Biology is a significantly more challenging class than Adam's previous science courses.
> *Dr. Stein:* I know. Adam has to understand how important this is. I think we need to push him a bit harder. I was just

like him at that age, but I learned to buckle down and I got through it. Adam can definitely do the same. He knows that he needs AP Bio on his transcript if he wants to get into a top university.

Principal: I think Adam is capable as well. It does seem that his interests are more in the areas of English and social studies. He is currently taking an AP English Lit and AP History course. Dropping AP Bio may help Adam succeed in those courses.

Dr. Stein: I just don't think so. Adam may not realize it now, but I see that he is going to be just like me. In the end he'll realize that Bio is the more important course for his future. If he does need to drop an AP, it will need to be English or History.

Dr. Stein is simply worrying about his son's future. He believes that the most promising career paths his son may choose will be better served by AP Bio than by a humanities course. He may even know that Adam's talents lie more in the sciences than in literature. But there may be something else at play here as well.

It is the same factor that is at play in most Little League games. We instinctively recoil as the overbearing parent next to us shouts "encouragement" (not usually of a positive sort) at their child, particularly after a strikeout or an error in the infield. Yet we know that we feel the same pull. When our child is up at bat, our stomachs are in knots, more nervous than if we were at the plate ourselves. We want our child to get that hit more than he himself wants it.

Or for those less athletically inclined, it may have been when our nine-year-old got herself dressed on Sunday morning and was ready to go off to play at her friend's. As she was about to run out the door, we could not help but ask, "Is that what you are going to wear?" Of course, the pink polka dot dress, green-striped sweater, and yellow rain boots were exactly what she planned to wear. And as she stepped out the door, we vowed that this would be the last time before her bat mitzva that she chooses her own clothes.

OVERLAPPING IDENTITIES

There is a common feature at the heart of all of these typical parental reactions. Well-meaning parents are concerned about their children's success. But mixed in together with that concern is an overlap of identity. Dr. Stein does not see himself as someone who drops AP Bio, that Little League mom would never allow herself to blow the big play, and very few of us could bear being seen in public in the stripy polka dot ensemble.

The visceral reaction we feel to our children's behavior stems more from what that behavior says about *us* than from what it means for our children. We often see our children as extensions of ourselves, and so their actions are a reflection of our own character. This perspective is quite natural. Our children are raised in our homes, learn our values, and may even resemble our physical appearance. In fact, seeing children as extensions of ourselves can greatly increase our feelings of love, caring, empathy, and patience

At the same time, we roll our eyes when we read Dr. Stein's conversation and grimace at the thought of the overbearing Little League or fashion-conscious parent. Watching someone else play the part of parent, we know instinctively that these are flawed reactions.

Why? We understand that the child's aptitude and self-image, not the parent's, should determine the appropriate expectations and guidance for that child. From a distance, and particularly when it pertains to someone else's child, we understand that parental decisions should be based on what the child needs. This is what it means to put the child at the center.

Despite our clarity regarding other people's children, this perspective is difficult to cultivate when it comes to our own families. Doing so requires us to consciously filter out visceral reactions that stem from our own concerns about identity or self-perception. It requires us to examine each decision we make to discern our true motivation. When we do so, our interactions may look more like one of these scenes from the Abram family.

WHOSE BAR MITZVA?

Sara and David Abram were up late again talking. This was becoming an unfortunate part of their routine. Jonny was their second son to begin preparations for his bar mitzva. His older brother Ben had gone through the process beautifully. Ben was not blessed with much of a singing voice, but he had put in the time, learned his Torah reading, prepared to lead the services, and written a short speech. Sara and David remembered the stress and work involved in those months of preparation for their older son, but they also remembered how proud they and Ben felt when it came time for the bar mitzva itself.

Now Jonny was just six weeks into his lessons and he had declared that he was done. He was willing to do *maftir*, a minimal part of the Torah reading, but he refused to learn the rest of the reading, and he absolutely would not lead the services or deliver any sort of speech.

David was angry when he found out. Jonny was a good boy, but this sort of laziness was unacceptable. Jonny was smart and capable, and there was no reason he could not pull this off just as well as his brother. Yet Jonny had never blatantly disobeyed his father before, and his refusal to go to bar mitzva lessons this past Sunday was so surprising that it caused David to hesitate.

Every night since Sunday, the Abrams had been up late trying to figure out what to do.

David: I think we should push him. I know that he can do this. He's just as smart and capable as Ben.

Sara: I'm not sure. Jonny doesn't usually push back like this. I wonder if he's scared of performing in front of a crowd.

David: You might be right. He's never wanted to lead any part of services on Shabbat. When he was little, he didn't even want to go up to the front for a lollipop. But won't he feel good at the end if we push him through this? Jonny won't be happy if he doesn't do what his brother did and what everyone in his class is doing.

Sara: Do you really think Jonny will be unhappy? Or is it really our pride that is at stake here? All those tuition dollars...and all of our guests will think he can't do this. I loved the look on my mom's face when Ben did such an impressive job, but I don't think we can force Jonny to do this for our own sake.

David: I definitely want Jonny to do this so that I won't be embarrassed when it comes time for his bar mitzva. But if it's really supposed to be his bar mitzva, I have to admit it does not seem fair to push him. He never has been someone who likes to perform in public.

Sara: I don't think we should go easy on him, though. Ben grew a lot because of the effort he put into his bar mitzva prep. If Jonny's not going to put the same hours into learning the Torah reading, we need to figure out some other way for him to grow.

David: Jonny's always liked helping Lisa with her homework. I wonder if he could do some tutoring at school. Perhaps we can ask the principal if we can set him up with a younger student who needs help with his Judaic studies. I still want Jonny to learn his Torah portion, but he can learn what it means. He doesn't need to learn how to read it aloud in shul.

Sara: That sounds great. I bet Jonny could even turn that into some sort of project. He loves working with his laptop. Maybe he could create an online program to help with the tutoring. If it goes well, Jonny may be proud enough that he will want to present that instead of the regular speech on Shabbat morning.

TURNING POINT

Some remarkable patterns emerge from this conversation. Of course, it seems like a great educational experience for Jonny to learn to read the full Torah portion. As a result, it would be easy for Sara and David to convince themselves that they want Jonny to do the full public reading for *his own* benefit. It might well be appropriate for parents to push another child despite the child's reluctance. But it is not right for Jonny, and the Abrams can see that.

How are the Abrams able to see this truth about their son? They truly view Jonny as an independent individual, with his own strengths, weaknesses, and preferences. As a result, they are able to separate his needs from their own and uncover what lies behind their initial desire to push him forward. Once they verbalize their own emotional needs to have Jonny put on a good show, they can turn their attention away from their needs to focus on what Jonny himself needs.

What happens once they have made this turn is striking. The Abrams see Jonny as an independent individual. They understand that it would not be right to force him to repeat his brother's bar mitzva pattern. However, this realization does not lead them to simply step back and allow Jonny to make his own choices without their guidance. Quite the opposite.

David and Sara turn away from their original plan and pursue a new idea, this time created with Jonny at the center.

They understand that forcing Jonny along the wrong path will be counterproductive, but they also know that as an independent individual, Jonny must be challenged and stimulated in order to grow and develop. Only Jonny himself can accomplish this growth. Their task, as his parents, is to inspire, motivate, and enable him to do so.

As we truly begin to put our children at the center, we learn that they are fundamentally independent individuals. We realize that we cannot direct or control them. Rather, we must understand who they are and enable them to grow toward our values. In the following chapters, we will explore what growth means and how we, as parents, can inspire, guide, and support it effectively.

Chapter Two

What Is Growth?

CHILDREN OR LITTLE ADULTS?

Dating back to the earliest paintings we have on record, depictions of children abound. Some are painted in religious scenes, others within nature, surrounded by family, or as single portraits. Regardless of the context, one striking common denominator emerges: If you look closely at the facial features and proportions of these "children," it becomes clear that the artist was in fact painting a mini-adult rather than a child.[1] The incongruity is so striking that some refer to the children in these paintings as "ugly Renaissance babies."

By the middle of the eighteenth century, artists had moved beyond this strange phenomenon. Children and babies are now painted with an understanding of their unique proportions, facial

---

1. For a full discussion of this phenomenon, see Mary Frances Duranti, *The Child in Seventeenth Century Dutch Painting*, Studies in the Fine Arts: Iconography VII (Ann Arbor, Mich: UMI Research Press, 1983). Art historians have debated the reasons for this phenomenon. See, for example, Lynda Pollock, *Forgotten Children: Parent-Child Relations from 1500 to 1900* (Cambridge: Cambridge University Press, 1983).

features, and expressions. The result, of course, seems so natural and appropriate that it is hard to understand how a genius like Rembrandt could have gotten it wrong.

Yet if we look at our own society, we may be surprised to see how often we make the same mistake.

Take, for example, the case of children's fashions. Stroll through any stylish children's store and you will see what appear to be very small adult mannequins wearing shrunken adult clothing. We are so used to these fashion statements that we see them as cute and natural. But it is not hard to imagine future historians wondering why we insisted that three-year-olds who cannot tell time wear fashionable watches, and children in diapers wear stylish jeans.

There is, of course, much current debate about issues of modesty and body image as these fashion trends apply to young girls.[2] But for us, the issue goes much deeper. These fashions do not just make a statement about dress or modesty. They are one of many modern examples that reveal our fundamental perspective on children and childhood.

For another example, visit the Little League version of your favorite sport: soccer, football, baseball, or basketball. For children as young as six or seven, games and leagues are set up to mirror the adult version of the sport. The more serious the league, the more the children at play look like miniature versions of professional athletes, down to the compression sleeves

---

2. Concerns about children's fashion trends are by no means new. For a historical perspective, see Iris Brooke, *English Children's Costume Since 1775* (London: A. & C. Black, 1930). More recently, the debate has hit the Internet fashion circuit at sites such as http://kidsfashion.about.com/od/designerstylesforkids/tp/adultdesignerlabelsforkids.htm and http://www.stylisheve.com/dressing-kids-like-adults-is-this-trend-in-or-should-it-be-on-the-way-out/ (accessed November 10, 2014).

worn by eight-year-old point guards and the $150 cleats for the ten-year-old pitcher.

ADULT EXPECTATIONS

We might argue the individual merits of fashion styles or youth sport training. However, these examples are just the tip of the iceberg in the pattern of how we treat children in the twenty-first century, and the way we see children may be more similar to the Renaissance artists' perspective than we would care to admit.

Think about the praise most often offered to children. We constantly laud them for adult-like thinking and encourage them to be more mature. Ugly paintings aside, we often want our children to act as much like grownups as possible. After all, adults are neater, quieter, and better-behaved (for the most part).

As well-meaning parents fall into this mistaken perception, we convince ourselves that by treating our children like adults, we are speeding their path toward maturity and success. In reality, just the opposite is true.

Remember punctual Dr. Stein? He is at synagogue at 8:45 a.m. every Shabbat morning. In what seems to be an example of good parenting, his sixteen-year-old son Adam is sitting right next to him. Yet if you look a bit closer, you will notice that Adam is scowling as he looks down at the closed siddur in his clenched fingers. Despite the look on Adam's face, Dr. Stein believes he is doing the right thing by forcing his son to come to synagogue with him, on time, each week.

Of course, we cannot say for certain whether Dr. Stein is making the best parenting decision. But it does seem as if he is painting with a Renaissance brush. If Adam is a mini-adult, then he should be pushed to conform to adult expectations. He should arrive in synagogue promptly and participate in the full service. The fact that Adam refuses to open his prayer book or let a smile cross his lips is a shortcoming by adult standards. Dr. Stein's solution? Continue to hold Adam to these expectations and in time the proper habits will take root.

Considering this pattern, we begin to notice the danger inherent in Dr. Stein's perspective. If we see children as mini-adults, we will be tempted to hold them to standards well beyond their capacity to achieve. At this point Dr. Stein might argue that if we place the bar high, our children will learn to jump.

Unfortunately, that is not the most probable result. As any parent of a teenager will tell you, it is far more likely that the child will eventually give up trying, grow frustrated and angry, or find some way around our expectations. In any of these scenarios, we will not be pleased with the results. In the area of religion, the possibility of our children ultimately rejecting our prematurely challenging expectations is particularly frightening.

A DEVELOPMENTAL PERSPECTIVE

When we judge our children as individuals at their own unique stage of development, we see a very different picture.

It is Shabbat morning and thirteen-year-old Jonny Abram is not sitting next to his father in synagogue. Jonny has quite a bit of energy, like many twelve-year-old boys. Mr. Abram would love to have his son by his side, but he recognizes that sitting quietly for three hours is not an appropriate expectation.

From his experience with his older son, Mr. Abram knows that working with young children can bring out the best in twelve-year-olds. The more lively pace of children's programming works perfectly with their energy, and their natural adolescent desire to feel a sense of control (if channeled properly) serves as a great motivator to lead. David Abram has arranged for Jonny to serve as one of his synagogue's youth group leaders. Jonny does an abridged prayer service himself, and then leads younger children in prayers, learning, and activities.

We could explain David's choice by emphasizing the fact that Jonny is *not* ready for the adult prayer service at his current stage of development. To do so, however, misses the most vital benefit of a developmental perspective. David does not look at Jonny and see what is missing. Rather, he looks at Jonny and sees the unique capacity inherent in Jonny's current stage of development. As a twelve-year-old, Jonny has the energy and the desire to lead a youth group in ways that an adult cannot. As a father, David's goal is to understand the unique capabilities that Jonny possesses today and enable him to use them to achieve a sense of success and fulfillment across all areas of his life.

In fact, our ability to view our children in a developmentally appropriate fashion may hinge most fundamentally on this point. This is more than a glass half-full/glass half-empty distinction. It determines whether we truly understand who our children are as their present selves.

THE CAPACITY OF CHILDREN

One of the best illustrations of this perspective comes in the extreme example of our youngest children. Think about a two-month-old baby. He cannot talk, walk, or crawl. If he is advanced, at most, he may have mastered rolling over. As a mini-adult, the baby seems to lack all capacity. He must be fed, changed, and cared for constantly. And so we begin to think that this is the entirety of the baby's essence. The baby simply lacks any unique capacity or capability.

Now watch what happens when the baby enters a room, makes eye contact, or smiles at any adult in the vicinity. That same incapable baby can elicit emotional reactions and generate a sense of caring and attention more effectively than most adults. Conventional wisdom assumes that the adult's reaction to the baby points only to the adult's feeling, which misses the crucial, active role that the baby plays in the interaction. The two-month-old has no abilities if judged by adult standards, but if judged in terms of developmental stage, he has a set of social skills with its own unique power.[3]

Apply this flipped perspective to other stages and other strengths will emerge: To your five-year-old, receiving a lollipop may be the highlight of a morning and constitute a true moment of joy. Losing a new toy, on the other hand, may be a true disaster that produces a state of distress. The five-year-old may feel similar intense sadness when dropped off at school by a parent, and overwhelming happiness when the parent returns.

As parents, we may be frustrated by what we see as our children's inability to control their emotions, whether these lead to bouts of tears and or to hyperactive excitement. By adult standards we are correct. In contrast, if we employ a developmentally appropriate lens, we can begin to appreciate the unique capacity for intense emotion and creative imagination that a five-year-old displays. It is not just that young children cannot control themselves. It is that in many ways they experience both the positive and the negative events in their lives more fully and intensely than we do as adults.[4]

---

3. The educational philosopher John Dewey makes this point strongly in his *Democracy and Education*, chap. 4, and expands on the broader perspective both there and in his other works, most notably *The School and Society*. We will see below that a similar perspective is shared by other developmental psychologists and educators such as Jean Piaget and Jerome Bruner.

4. The noted educator Rabbi Shlomo Wolbe makes similar recommendations for appropriate developmental expectations and gives a striking depiction of the intensity of a child's imaginative play as well as its implications for education. See his *Planting and Building: Raising a Jewish Child* (Jerusalem: Feldheim, 1999), 21–23.

A decade later, the same child may come home at the end of the day filled mostly with complaints. At fifteen, the child sees clearly that teachers are absolutely unfair, the principal is obviously a hypocrite, and adults (including parents) are generally incompetent. Teens are quite certain that they could do better.

The frustrating aspect of dealing with teens is clear, and they are indeed infuriating when judged by adult standards. Here too, though, if we employ a developmentally appropriate lens, we can see a unique teenage capacity to pursue justice without compromise. We can also understand the power of teenagers' belief in their ability to impact their world. It is not just that they are arrogant, it is that they truly believe in their power to do better than the current status quo.

The developmental lens is not just a romantic view of childhood or a poetic reassurance to exasperated parents. Rather, it is a sincere appraisal of the inherent skills and capacities of each stage of childhood. This perspective helps us have more patience with our children. It also enables us to generate age-appropriate expectations that increase the likelihood of our children's success.

SUPPORTING GROWTH

The ultimate value of this perspective goes well beyond these benefits. By recognizing the unique capacity our children hold at their current stage, we can use these capacities to help them grow to the next stage in their development. As they move from stage to stage, our children can integrate each of these skill sets within their ever-evolving personalities, thus enriching their full capacity.

To understand what this means in practice, let's return to Jonny Abram's Shabbat morning routine.

David Abram is pleased to see how gratified his son Jonny is when running a youth group. Mr. Abram is particularly happy that Jonny gets up without any trouble each Shabbat morning, happily and willingly going to synagogue. David Abram has had enough experience parenting to know that he should appreciate it when things are going smoothly. But he also knows that he needs to take advantage of this opportunity. What Jonny enjoys doing each Shabbat morning is wonderful now, but his synagogue experience needs to continue developing over the coming years. How can Jonny's energy bring him to the next stage?

Mr. Abram has been thinking about this for several weeks when he passes by a sign advertising a new Friday night "Carlebach minyan" in his neighborhood. David himself is not particularly fond of the extra singing and dancing that accompanies this sort of service, but it strikes him that it may be just the right match for Jonny. It takes a few Friday nights to warm up, but soon Jonny is right in the fray, singing and dancing and enjoying the prayer service.

Depending on Jonny's personality, one can just as easily imagine Mr. Abram having taken another approach. He might have helped Jonny channel his desire for control to take a leading role in the prayers at synagogue, joining the main service to help lead the portions appropriate for his age. Alternatively, David could have channeled that same desire for control and success toward helping Jonny develop activities to teach the kids in his youth group about how to pray.

Whatever path Mr. Abram chooses, the essential point remains the same: Because he understands Jonny's current capacity, David can help Jonny use this capacity to grow and broaden his abilities, integrating the unique capacities of each given age within an ever-expanding framework of competence.

MINI-SCIENTISTS

We have seen how David Abram invests significant effort in planning for his son's ongoing growth in this sphere. Yet we must be absolutely clear that David's work is focused on setting the scene, arranging experiences, and adjusting expectations. He is the facilitator of his son's growth, but only Jonny himself can actually grow.

The preferred metaphor of the Swiss psychologist Jean Piaget, whose pioneering work in developmental psychology we will soon explore, may be helpful in centering our perspective. Piaget was fond of describing children as mini-scientists. Give young children any new object or place them in a new situation and they will immediately start to "experiment." How children experiment will depend on their age; babies will test the properties of an object by tasting it, a two-year-old may bang it on the floor, and a four-year-old will be sophisticated enough to manipulate the object, turn knobs, press buttons, and use it in a number of imaginative ways.

The experimentation does not stop as the child gets older. Teenagers experiment just the same, only not with physical objects. Instead, they see how parents, friends, and teachers respond when their buttons are pressed. The teens themselves may not be aware of why or how they are testing, but they, too, are taking the role of mini-scientist as they attempt to decipher the world around them. It is this process of research and experimentation that leads to their ongoing growth.

David Abram saw Jonny as the experimenter. And so David naturally began to look for what tools his son had at his disposal. David's goal was to arrange the lab such that Jonny could effectively use his tools. His decisions about how Jonny should spend Shabbat morning provided a laboratory well suited for his son. By carefully structuring the environment to match his son's capacity, David set out the conditions that would enable Jonny to grow.[5]

---

5. John Dewey sees the setting of conditions for growth as the primary task of any educator. See *Democracy and Education*, chap. 4.

COGNITIVE DEVELOPMENT

The evolution of children's capacity to make sense of their world is not simply anecdotal. Over a hundred years ago, Jean Piaget formulated four stages of a child's cognitive development from birth through pre-teen. In doing so, he founded a stream of psychological research focused on understanding children's development. Later researchers have built on Piaget's work, adding stages following those that he created or further examining the way children move from one stage to the next.[6]

Before we look at the stages themselves, we must be aware that they are merely a general guideline. No theory of development accounts perfectly for the full range of human growth, and no individual child can be adequately described by one of Piaget's stages. While ignorance of developmental stages can mislead us, too much reliance on these theories can cause us to reduce a child to an overly simplified label.

For our purposes, the stages are not intended to be the ultimate description of the child. Rather, they can guide us and orient our perspective to identify a child's capacity at each age. We will use Piaget's stages as an example to illustrate what we can learn from the stages.[7]

---

6. We cite Piaget's stages as one example. For an alternative psychological account of child development, see Lev Vygotsky, *Mind in Society: The Development of Higher Psychological Processes* (Cambridge, Mass.: Harvard University Press, 1978). Vygotsky preferred to describe children's growth as a steady unfolding, as opposed to discrete stages. Like Vygotsky, Jerome Bruner suggests a developmental model with important differences from Piaget's approach; see his *Studies in Cognitive Growth* (New York: John Wiley, 1966). For older teens and adults, Robert Kegan suggests a more complex interplay of stage development, which extends well into adulthood. See his *The Evolving Self: Problem and Process in Human Development* (Cambridge, Mass.: Harvard University Press, 1983) and *In Over Our Heads: The Mental Demands of Modern Life* (Cambridge, Mass.: Harvard University Press, 1998).

7. The most complete resource on Piaget's writing and research is www.piaget.org, which includes stage summaries together with extensive biographical and bibliographical materials.

Sensorimotor (up to age 2): The child learns by making movements and experiencing the resulting sensations. He acquires knowledge only through concrete information, assimilating it into existing schema and gradually expanding the schema to accommodate new data. During this stage, children learn that they exist separately from the objects around them, and that such objects continue to exist even when not visible.

Preoperational (ages 2 to 7): The child develops the skill of direct representation, learning that symbols (words or pictures) correspond to objects. He can also understand simple counting and classification schemes centered around concrete, present reality, but cannot accommodate more than one perspective, such as classifying a blue circle as both blue and a circle. In Piaget's famous test, the child will predict that a tall narrow glass contains a greater volume than an equivalent short and wide glass. Similarly, the child is unable to understand that others have different perspectives and, therefore, the child is fundamentally self-centered.

Concrete Operational (ages 7 to 11): The child begins to create logical structures to explain physical experiences. For example, the child can now understand basic mathematical equations and can predict that if $2 + 3 = 5$ then $5 - 3 = 2$. He can also understand that the volume of liquid in a short, wide cup may be the same as in a tall, narrow cup. Thanks to these logical structures, the child can begin to understand alternative points of view and imagine the perspectives of others. However, the child's structures are still generally tied to concrete reality, which limits the range of empathic capacity.

Formal Operational (ages 11 to 15): This final stage, which begins around puberty, is fundamentally similar to the mental operations of an adult. The child can formulate fully abstract ideas, including theoretical hypotheses and deductions. Mathematical reasoning expands beyond numerical to algebraic logic. Interpersonally, the child now has the mental capacity to imagine a full range of perspectives, including ones not actually encountered.

Being aware of these stages forces us to realize that our children possess different capacities at different ages. More importantly, these stages complement the general capacities we identified earlier (e.g., Jonny's energy) by drilling beneath the surface. Piaget did not just identify children's tendencies or personal characteristics. He highlighted the mental structures that underlie all of their thinking at a given stage.

Most of us are not used to thinking about the concept of cognitive structures. These are not pieces of content knowledge, skills, or abilities that wax or wane depending on practice. It is impossible to skip over a cognitive developmental stage, and short of serious mental illness there will be no backsliding.

A mental structure is better compared to a physical characteristic such as height. It may develop over time, but it does not respond directly to intervention. At least according to Piaget, trying to change a child's cognitive developmental stage makes about as much sense trying to change the child's shoe size.

What can understanding cognitive development mean for us as parents?

Back when Rachel Stein was five years old, she was solidly in the preoperational stage. One night at dinner, she got very upset that her brother Adam had a larger cup than she did. There were many ways to deal with this situation, but Piaget makes it quite clear that explaining to Rachel that she does have the same amount of milk would not have been an effective approach. Even if Rachel's mom could get her to *say* she understood, Rachel was physically incapable of grasping this abstract concept. Debbie Stein may have obtained compliance, but she would not have obtained understanding.

Piaget also teaches us that asking Adam to understand his sister's perspective would have been equally unhelpful. Nine-year-old Adam had moved to the concrete operational stage. He could indeed understand that others have different perspectives. Yet, as he was still tied to his own direct experience, Adam would not be able to empathize with Rachel's preoperational reality. Put differently, Adam could not fathom that Rachel truly believed she has less milk. (In truth, this concept is challenging even for adults at the formal operations stage.) Adam may have submitted out of self-interest, but he did not have the capacity to empathize with preoperational Rachel.

On the other hand, it was more likely that Adam could have understood his mother's perspective. He had personal experience with whining children, and he could have imagined how his mother felt as Rachel demanded the taller cup. Whether Adam wanted to help his mother would have depended on many other factors. But if she approached the request in a way that Adam had the cognitive tools to comprehend, Debbie would have stood a chance of enabling him to empathize rather than just obey.

Cognitive developmental stages enable us to see how our children see the world and give us the tools to communicate with them in ways that they can fundamentally comprehend. Combine this basic awareness of cognitive development with an intuitive sense of our children's unique capacities at each stage and you will never mistake your child for a mini-adult.

Beyond math problems or milk at dinner, cognitive development determines how our children learn to be good people and good Jews. Understanding the realms of moral and religious development, which we will soon explore, will give us the tools to support this even more crucial area of growth.

Chapter Three

Morals and Mitzvot

Cognitive development is important, vital even. Yet when we think about good parenting, our considerations turn more toward the kind of people we want our children to become than to how we want their cognitive structures to develop.

What is the connection between the ability to compute algebra problems and the capacity to treat others kindly?

Let's go back to Rachel Stein's bat mitzva party to explore. It is a beautiful event, and the Steins are so proud of all the work their daughter has put into her preparations. But as they look over to her table now, they see that Rachel has managed to arrange things so that only her small clique can be near her. The other girls in the class have been relegated to an external circle. Looking at the other girls' faces, Debbie Stein is quite sure they understand what Rachel has done.

For her part, Debbie does not understand how this happened. She and her husband were clear in their messages to Rachel. Rachel knew she had to invite all the girls in her class to join her.

And she knew that she was supposed to treat them all kindly. Mrs. Stein had even taken the time to explain to her daughter that this is what it means to be a good hostess. This is what it means to be a bat mitzva.

Clearly, though, Rachel had either not understood or not accepted her parents' message. She is happily chatting with her chosen clique, and seems oblivious to the feelings of her other guests.

The Steins are frustrated. Why doesn't Rachel get it?

MORAL DEVELOPMENT

Armed with Jean Piaget's stage-development theory, we may already have intuited the answer. If Rachel has not fully progressed to the formal operational stage, she may not yet have developed the cognitive ability to take the perspective of another person.

Rachel heard her parents and followed their instructions: she did invite all the girls in her class. What Rachel cannot do, however, is shift her own perspective from a self-centered cognitive viewpoint to one that is empathetic. A twelve-year-old child will naturally see herself as the sun, with all others orbiting around her. Her needs and desires are central, not because she is selfish, but because, in her understanding of the world, that is simply logical. Everything she observes and all of her reactions make perfect sense from this point of view.

Even when we begin to see that Rachel's behavior may be developmentally appropriate, we can still understand why the Steins are exasperated. How can they teach their daughter that she is not the center of the universe? Just ask Copernicus what it takes to shift someone away from this perspective.

Yet once we understand the cognitive roots of the problem, more effective strategies do present themselves. We began to uncover just such a strategy at the end of Chapter 2 with our suggestion for how Mrs. Stein could enlist Adam's help in giving his sister the larger cup. To give the Steins more potent advice, however, we need to enlist the assistance of another developmental psychologist, Lawrence Kohlberg.[1]

LAWRENCE KOHLBERG

Working at Harvard for over three decades, Kohlberg translated Piaget's understanding of cognitive development into a theory of moral development. He deepens our understanding of how the cognitive structures identified by Piaget are also the logic for moral decision-making of the kind we saw Rachel engage in during her bat mitzva. Kohlberg's theory enables us to see not just how our children think, but specifically how they think about the questions that matter most.

To orient ourselves, let's take a brief look at Kohlberg's stages. Kohlberg divides the moral development of the individual into three fundamental levels of moral reasoning, each of which is subdivided into two stages.[2]

Preconventional Level

Children at this level cannot see beyond their own personal needs and desires.

---

1. Kohlberg's work occupied center stage in discussions of morality and moral development for three decades. Of course, he did have his detractors. One of the most pointed critiques comes from Carol Gilligan, who suggests that there is a significant gender bias in Kohlberg's research. See Gilligan's seminal *In a Different Voice* (Cambridge: Harvard University Press, 1993). Her conclusions were translated into a philosophical perspective by Nel Noddings, *Caring* (Berkeley: University of California Press, 1984).
2. Our portrayal of these six stages is based on Kohlberg's formulation in *Psychology of Moral Development*, vol. 2, *Essays in Moral Development* (San Francisco: Harper & Row, 1984), 174–76. Note that Kohlberg's stages do not correspond to age groupings as neatly as Piaget's.

Stage 1: Heteronomous morality

Children in this stage obey rules simply to avoid physical punishment or property damage. They are entirely focused on their own interests.

Stage 2: Individualism and exchange

Children in this stage can follow rules that are to their own immediate benefit. They begin to see that each person has distinct individual interests to pursue, and they try to serve their own needs while allowing others to do the same. A child in this stage is particularly interested in concrete ideas of fairness and "you scratch my back, I'll scratch yours" exchanges.

Conventional Level

Children at this level understand that they are members of a larger communal or societal group.

Stage 3: Roles and relationships

Children in this stage try to live up to the expectations of people to whom they are close, as well as to the expectations tied to the various social roles they occupy (son, daughter, brother, sister, etc.). They want to live up to what is expected of a "good boy" or a "good girl." Shared feelings, mutual relationships, and trust are primary in their moral decision-making.

Stage 4: Social system

Children in this stage take the perspective of the system rather than of the individual. They emphasize upholding the rules of the system and are concerned with contributing to society. When asked why stealing is wrong, they will reply that it would undermine the system, asking, "What would happen if everyone did that?"

Postconventional or Principled Level

Individuals at this level look past the norms and laws of society to fundamental ethical principles.[3]

Stage 5: Social contract

Children in the social contract stage no longer see the laws of society as the ultimate authority and instead understand them as binding only because they have been jointly agreed upon.[4] The social contract is formulated according to utilitarian principles: the greatest good for the greatest number.

Stage 6: Universal ethical principles

At the final stage in Kohlberg's trajectory, individuals evaluate their moral decisions based on universal moral principles such as justice and equality. These moral principles, and not the social contract, lend authority to societal rules and norms. As a result, the individual feels bound to obey only those rules that accord with the universal principles of natural law.[5]

---

3. Throughout his research, Kohlberg identified very few individuals who had reached this level of moral development. These stages will obviously be the least relevant for our parenting concerns, but we have included them for the sake of completeness.

4. The notion of social contract is expressed well by the social institution of marriage. Two persons who decide to get married accept certain duties and obligations to one another. These duties and obligations are binding because the two persons entering into the contract (in this case, marriage) willingly agree to them.

5. Kohlberg often points to Martin Luther King Jr. as a salient example of Stage 6 morality, which differentiates man's law from higher, or natural, law. In his "Letter from a Birmingham Jail," King explicitly states that in order to be "just," "human law" must be "rooted in eternal law and natural law." Any human law that disregards natural law must be proclaimed unjust and civilly disobeyed. Quoted in Kohlberg, *Philosophy of Moral Development*, 43. We may not agree with Kohlberg's underlying philosophy, but his analysis of cognitive moral development nonetheless remains a relevant guidepost. For a full discussion of this question, see Barry Kislowicz,

APPLYING THE THEORY

We can now turn back to Rachel and her frustrated parents. With Kohlberg's moral stages in mind, it is easier to understand how Rachel perceives this scenario.

Based on her age and behavior, Rachel is most likely in Stage 2 or 3 of her moral development. Assuming that Rachel is functioning within a Stage 2 paradigm, we know that she will understand moral questions through an instrumental, self-interested lens. To be clear, this does not mean that she will make the wrong decision in each case. It means that whatever decision she does make will be motivated by Stage 2 factors such as concrete ideas of fairness, even exchange, and mutual benefit. Kohlberg's stages highlight the method of reasoning we use to reach moral decisions, not whether the decisions themselves are morally correct.[6]

Dan and Debbie Stein had a talk with Rachel before her bat mitzva. They talked to her about being kind to the other girls and understanding how they would feel if they were excluded. Unfortunately, none of those messages are relevant to a Stage 2 perspective. If, on the other hand, the Steins had talked to Rachel about treating her friends fairly or, better yet, about including Rebecca because Rebecca had included Rachel at her party last week, they would have at least been speaking a language that Rachel could understand.

Alternatively, if Rachel functions within a Stage 3 perspective, the Steins must be aware that relationships are a primary factor in

---

Appropriating Kohlberg for Traditional Jewish High Schools (New York: Teachers College Press, 2004).

6. Kohlberg argues that by Stage 5 and Stage 6, individuals will have progressed to a mode of reasoning so advanced that their decisions will be, on the whole, ethically appropriate. However, in Kohlberg's research very few individuals ever reach these advanced stages. If a person does progress to this advanced level, it will certainly be as a fully mature adult.

her moral decisions. Being loyal to those with whom she already feels a sense of friendship will be a more powerful pull than the abstract imperative to be kind to everyone. They will be fighting an uphill battle in asking Rachel to treat her other classmates the same way she treats her good friends, but if they realize that Rachel is using Stage 3 logic, they will at least understand what pulls her in this direction.

On the other hand, Rachel's desire to fulfill expectations related to her roles may be a more helpful factor at this stage. The Steins would do well to talk to her about what a "good hostess" would do in this scenario. They may even integrate their discussion within a larger discussion about Rachel's new role as a young Jewish woman, and the responsibilities that come with being a bat mitzva.

HEINZ'S DILEMMA

It is clear that the arguments that work in Stage 2 will fall flat in Stage 3, and those that work in Stage 3 are premature for Stage 2. How are the Steins to know where Rachel stands?

Here Kohlberg's research methods may be even more helpful than his stage theory. Kohlberg assessed moral-stage progress by asking children to respond to a moral story such as the classic Heinz dilemma:

> A woman was near death from a special kind of cancer. There was one drug that the doctors thought might save her. It was a form of radium that a druggist in the same town had recently discovered. The drug was expensive to make, but the druggist was charging ten times what the drug cost him to produce. He paid $200 for the radium and charged $2,000 for a small dose of the drug. The sick woman's husband, Heinz, went to everyone he knew to borrow the money, but he could only get together about $1,000, which is half of what it cost.

He told the druggist that his wife was dying and asked him to sell it cheaper or let him pay later. But the druggist said: "No, I discovered the drug and I'm going to make money from it." So Heinz got desperate and broke into the man's laboratory to steal the drug for his wife. Should Heinz have broken into the laboratory to steal the drug for his wife? Why or why not?[7]

In categorizing the responses to this tale, Kohlberg's researchers paid attention to whether the respondent believed Heinz should steal the drug. However, they paid greater attention to how the respondent justified the response. It was this justification that enabled researchers to determine the respondent's stage of moral development.

Heinz's dilemma, of course, is a well-crafted moral quandary. However, similar moral dilemmas occur multiple times every day for all of our children. If the Steins listen closely as they talk with their daughter around the dinner table, they will soon see evidence of her moral reasoning. Like the researchers, they must pay attention not only to what Rachel reports but to how she describes her thought process.

She is upset at her friend Rebecca and will not talk to her, but why? She thinks her math teacher did not treat her fairly, but what does "fair" mean?

The Steins may not use Kohlberg's official scoring guide, but if they listen carefully, they will soon begin to hear *how* Rachel thinks about the decisions she makes every day. This is not something the Steins can accomplish the week before Rachel's bat

---

7. Lawrence Kohlberg, *Essays on Moral Development*, vol. I, *The Philosophy of Moral Development* (San Francisco: Harper & Row, 1981).

mitzva. It is an ongoing effort over months and years, which will enable them to speak in language that Rachel understands.[8]

THE IMPACT OF DISCUSSION

Something even more important happened as Kohlberg's researchers talked with children about moral dilemmas. They began to realize that discussing moral dilemmas actually changed the way children thought. In fact, they observed a measurable acceleration in moral development in children who were regularly engaged in these discussions.[9] And so, while Piaget believed that trying to accelerate cognitive development is futile, Kohlberg proved that how we talk to our children can actually change the way they develop.[10]

This can take place in a classroom with trained teachers, or it can happen in a simple conversation like the one Sara Abram had with her nine-year-old daughter Lisa during their drive to school.

> *Lisa:* Mom...I'm not feeling good. My stomach hurts.
> *Sara:* Lisa, you seemed fine earlier this morning at breakfast. Is something bothering you? Do you think we need to go to the doctor?
> *Lisa:* No. I'm just nervous about school today. I want to play with Hana and her friends during recess, and they won't let

---

8. In truth, this is only one of the many benefits of listening carefully to our children. In the coming chapters we will explore more fully the powerful effects of conversation on our children's growth.
9. Moshe Blatt and Lawrence Kohlberg, "The Effects of Classroom Moral Discussion upon Children's Level of Moral Judgment," *Journal of Moral Education* 4, no. 2 (1975): 129–61.
10. Kohlberg has good company in this perspective. The leading psychologists Jerome Bruner and Lev Vygotsky both felt that careful adult intervention can speed cognitive development. See *The Collected Works of L. S. Vygotsky* (New York: Plenum, 1987) and Jerome S. Bruner et al., "Language and Experience," in *John Dewey Reconsidered*, ed. R. S. Peters (London: Routledge & Kegan Paul, 1977).

my other friend, Danielle, play with them too. I really want
to play with them, but I don't want Danielle to be mad at me.
Sara: What do you think you're going to decide?
Lisa: I think I am going to play with Hana today. I play with
Danielle most days. It's not fair if I have to miss out on playing with Hana. I'll let Danielle sit next to me on the bus ride
home to make up for it.
Sara: I understand. You've been good friends with Danielle
for years, and you just met Hana recently. What do you think
a good friend would do?

Note that Sara does not tell Lisa what to do. Rather, she
questions her daughter's logic. Lisa may or may not decide to
leave Hana behind, but even in this snippet of a conversation,
Sara challenges her daughter's mode of thinking by presenting an
alternative rationale. This sort of questioning and discussion will
ultimately give Lisa the tools to confront more complex dilemmas
and make better decisions.

Of course, understanding what to do may not always
translate into acting out the right choices in practice. As many of
us learned in our own youth, knowing is half the battle.[11] We will
return to the question of action, the second half of the battle, in
Part II of this book.

WHAT ABOUT GOD?

Fights between friends, difficulties in getting along with siblings,
and disagreements with teachers are challenges that all children
must navigate. Yet when Jewish parents think about the kind of
people they hope their children will become, their thoughts span

---

11. Some readers may find it surprising, but the original source for this widespread saying
is the 1989 *G.I.Joe* cartoon series by Marvel Productions.

well beyond the interpersonal realm to include questions of faith and religious commitment.

Piaget helped us see what our children can understand. Kohlberg enabled us to comprehend how they view their interactions with others. To complete the circle, we must uncover how they relate to God, Torah, and mitzvot throughout their development.

Developmental psychologists have shown that faith development proceeds along a very similar continuum to the development stages we have already seen. For the purposes of broad academic inquiry, "faith" is defined as the way an individual gives meaning to the major forces surrounding and affecting her life.[12]

For us, of course, faith development will be more closely and specifically connected to the way our children relate to God. As we look to the religious realm more specifically, earlier sources from within our own tradition predicted much of what developmental psychologists later discovered.

MAIMONIDES ON MOTIVATION

Talmud Torah keneged kulam, the study of Torah, is regarded as among the most valuable of religious actions. Even more than prayer, Torah study is seen as a central indicator of a Jew's relationship with God.[13] Regarding the motivation for Torah study, Maimonides, in the twelfth century, wrote:

> Imagine a small child who has been brought to his teacher so that he may be taught the Torah…. The teacher may say, "Read and I will give you some nuts or figs; I will give you a bit of honey." With this motivation, the child tries to

---

12. James W. Fowler, *Stages of Faith* (New York: Harper & Row, 1981).
13. Mishna Pe'ah 1:1.

read. He does not work hard for the sake of reading itself, since he does not understand its value. He reads in order to obtain the food.

As his intelligence improves…the child will set his desire upon something of greater value. Then his teacher may say to him: "Learn this passage or this chapter, and I will give you a coin or two." Again he will try to read in order to receive the money, since money is more important to him than study…

As his intelligence improves still more…the child will set his desire to something more dignified. Then his teacher may say to him: "Learn so that you can be a leader and a judge, and people will honor you and stand before you like so-and-so." And he will read and learn to achieve this degree, with the end in his mind being the honor that others will give him and the praise he will receive.[14]

This progression should be very familiar to us. The child moves from seeking concrete physical rewards, to the symbolic reward of money, and ultimately to a non-physical reward of honor. Yet, in the service of God, this cannot be the final destination. As the individual's development continues, he will ultimately understand that:

The end of wisdom is neither to acquire honor from other men nor to earn more money. One ought not to busy oneself with God's Torah in order to earn one's living by it; nor should the end of studying wisdom be anything but

14. Maimonides, *Commentary on the Mishna*, Introduction to Perek Helek, translation from http://www.mhcny.org/qt/1005.pdf (accessed March 3, 2015). In their original context, these words address the larger question of serving God for the sake of reward, but taken on their own they also support our efforts.

knowing it. The truth has no other purpose than knowing that it is truth. Since the Torah is truth, the purpose of
knowing it is to do it.

Maimonides himself notes that it is unseemly to offer our children physical rewards for learning Torah. Yet, given the nature
of the human condition, it is unavoidable. If we understand our
children's level of development, we can offer them developmentally appropriate motivation and guidance to engage in religious
action (e.g., learning).

Engagement in religious action will itself help speed their
growth to more complex stages of religious development. As the
Talmud exhorts, "a person should always involve himself with
Torah and mitzvot even not for their own sake, since through this
involvement he will come to involve himself with them for their
own sake."[15]

FAITH DEVELOPMENT

While Maimonides specifically addresses the question of
motivation, we must think about the entirety of our children's
relationships with God. How, for example, would we approach
a situation like the one unfolding below in the Abrams' home?

Ben Abram has just returned home from his school's Holocaust Remembrance Day program. Together with his fellow tenth-
graders, Ben was charged with putting together the high school
program. Learning about the Holocaust is always difficult, but
in the past, it has never particularly bothered Ben on a religious
level. This year is different, though, and his mother, Sara, knows it
as soon as Ben walks in the door. He mopes around silently until
midway through dinner. Picking at his food, he mutters to no one

---

15. Nazir 23b.

in particular, "How could God let that happen? Those people didn't deserve it."

Sara and her husband, David, quickly look across the table, each of them hoping the other knows how to respond to Ben's question.

If we have learned something from this chapter, we know that before Sara or David responds to Ben, they must be sure they understand his question. The words are simple enough. But we can only discern the true nature of the underlying concern if we know how Ben perceives the world around him. In other words, we cannot talk to Ben about how God could let this happen if we do not know how Ben understands God.[16]

Paralleling the cognitive development of Piaget and the moral development of Kohlberg, Harvard psychologist James Fowler lays out six stages of faith development.[17] Like Piaget and Kohlberg, Fowler's focus is not on *what* children believe but on *how* they formulate and understand their faith at each stage. In Fowler's scheme, children from age six through the early teens see the world through a "mythic-literal faith" (Stage 2). They rely heavily on faith stories to explain how the world works. These stories are taken literally. Most important for our case, children in this stage value authority and rules over personal perspective.

As they move into adolescence, children transition into a "synthetic-conventional faith" (Stage 3). They can see additional layers of meaning within their faith stories, and they begin to

---

16. Of course, none of us can truly claim to understand God. But each of us relates to God based on the best of our understanding. The question for Ben's parents is how does he, at age fifteen, understand God.

17. For a full description of these stages, see Fowler's *Stages of Faith*, cited above, n. 12. Many helpful summaries are readily available online.

synthesize these stories into a cohesive faith perspective. As a result, they are particularly bothered by inconsistencies. Teens at this stage are focused on identity formation, and they begin to claim their faith as their own.

Knowing nothing else about Ben, we are immediately struck by two realizations. First, what is an appropriate response for Stage 2 Ben would be a completely inappropriate for Stage 3 Ben (and vice versa). Second, knowing that Ben is likely on the cusp of transition from Stage 2 to Stage 3, we would absolutely expect him to begin asking this sort of question. As part of his cognitive development, Ben is struggling to create a cohesive picture from all the religious teachings he has heard over the years, and he is struggling to claim this picture as part of his own identity. Questions of this sort are as natural as his recent growth spurt and his acne.

So how should Sara and David respond?

Unfortunately, we do not yet have the answer for them. In Chapter 1, we learned that the best response to a child's question is not necessarily an answer. We have now gained additional background by understanding Ben's cognitive, moral, and faith development. But we can't possibly respond to Ben until we get to know who *he* is on a more nuanced, personal level.

We will now turn our attention to the task of delving beyond developmental theory, to explore the individual personalities of our children. Ultimately, it is this exploration that will equip us to respond meaningfully to Ben.

Chapter Four

Learning Your Child

How do the Abrams get to know Ben? How can we each develop a deep understanding of our children?

The vital groundwork for this effort comes from what we learned in Chapter 1. As parents, we tend to intermingle our own identities with those of our children.

Think back to that Little League parent whose self-esteem is tied up with her child's next at-bat. The child at the plate is an extension of herself, and his performance somehow affects her even more directly than her own.

Remember Sara and David's discussion about their son Jonny's upcoming bar mitzva? When they started thinking about what was good for *him*, and not what they themselves wanted, they were able to determine how to guide him. We can begin learning our children only once we have firmly established that they are indeed unique, independent individuals.

A VITAL CAVEAT

Seeing our children as extensions of ourselves is one key stumbling block in our attempt to learn who they are themselves. But there is a different type of error that most of us find just as challenging to overcome.

Imagine it's Monday morning and you are watching a group of twelve-year-olds eating lunch in their school cafeteria. Rachel, the brown-haired girl at the end of the table, is talking throughout. Gesticulating energetically, she seems to have the other children wrapped up in her stories. Rachel is so busy socializing that she barely has time to eat her own lunch. She pauses when a new girl walks up to the table, invites the girl to sit next to her, and continues her story-telling.

Intrigued by Rachel's gregarious behavior, you return to the school cafeteria on Tuesday, and you see an almost identical scene. Some of the children have changed seats, but Rachel remains in the center of the discussion. This time she is conducting what seems to be an extensive interview with the new girl, introducing her to the others and sharing all the information this girl will need to know about her new school.

If I asked you to tell me what you have learned about Rachel, you would confidently tell me that she is an outgoing, charismatic, and sociable girl. Any further observations you conducted at her school would confirm your assessment.

But what would happen if you now observed Rachel in her summer camp dining hall, at her home dinner table, or even later that same day during afternoon recess? Most of us would expect to see the same extroverted girl at work. Yet the truth may be quite different. Rachel may well be outgoing during school lunch, shy at summer camp, and a bookworm during afternoon recess.

This is a jarring realization. As humans, we are built to analyze, interpret, and make sense of the world around us. When we observe Rachel's behavior, especially if that behavior is repeated, we draw conclusions about her personality and essential disposition.

If our conclusions were correct, we would expect to see the same disposition on display in another setting. Yet as research shows, time and again, that is simply not the case. Psychologists call our tendency to jump to mistaken conclusions a fundamental attribution error.[1]

CHARACTER OR SITUATION?

Disposition varies with setting. And not only disposition. Beginning in the 1920s, psychologists showed that character traits such as honesty and integrity did not hold steady from one situation to another. Children who might cheat in one setting would act honestly in another, depending more on context than on their individual character.[2]

Despite the evidence, most of us have great difficulty avoiding the fundamental attribution error. When it comes to our observations of Rachel, that is an unfortunate but not terribly dangerous mistake. Our conclusions may be misguided, but if we watch long enough, Rachel will go on to prove us wrong.

---

1. See Malcolm Gladwell's *The Tipping Point* (New York: Back Bay, 2002) and his essay "The New-Boy Network," http://gladwell.com/the-new-boy-network/ (accessed June 17, 2015), where he quotes Theodore Newcomb's research on extroverted behavior among boys in a summer camp setting. Newcomb's research provides the basis for our fictional anecdote.

2. The most influential of these studies are reported in Hugh Hartshorne and Mark A. May, *Studies in the Nature of Character* (New York: Macmillan, 1928).

Committing the fundamental attribution error with our own children, however, can have more significant consequences.

RAMIFICATIONS

At the Steins' dinner table, Rachel is the youngest in the family. Food is served, and often inhaled, by her older brother Adam, who immediately launches into stories from his day, recounting his triumphs and complaints to their parents. Rachel tries desperately to follow the conversation, but she rarely even attempts to get a word in edgewise. When Dan Stein asks his daughter about her day, she is so exhausted that she responds in monosyllables.

As we did earlier, the Steins come to a conclusion about Rachel. Seeing her act this way each night at dinner, they are convinced that Rachel is a shy, socially reluctant girl. The problem is that, unlike us, they are not just casual observers. They interact with Rachel on a daily basis, and their interactions with her will be framed by this mistaken assessment of her personality

As a result, they are liable to react in a misguided manner when they hear reports from other contexts. When Rachel's principal first calls with concerns that Rachel may be excluding another girl in her class, the Steins will be unlikely to take her comments seriously. Shy Rachel excluding others? If Rachel had friends at all, that would be wonderful!

Similarly, the Steins' own efforts may be inappropriate. They may devote effort to helping Rachel learn social skills, encouraging her to socialize more on weekends, setting up play-dates, or the like. There is nothing inherently negative about any of these efforts, but Rachel herself will intuit that her parents feel she is fundamentally shy. She may know that her parents misunderstand her and become frustrated with their perception.

Even more likely, Rachel may unwittingly live up (or down) to her parents' expectations, and this is the tragedy of a fundamental attribution error. Parents jump to conclusions about their children, and these conclusions become a self-fulfilling prophecy that limits the child's growth.

To make matters worse, think about how this unfolds over the years. Assume for a moment that the Steins' conclusions about Rachel's personality are correct today. Will they be correct six months or six years from now?

LEARNING, NOT KNOWING

This is why we purposely talk about *learning* our children and not *knowing* our children. The first lesson of learning our children is that we must always bear in mind that we do not have the full picture. Of course, we never have the full picture when it comes to another person. Each individual is, by definition, more complex, nuanced, and multifaceted than another can completely comprehend.

When it comes to children, however, we are most likely to fool ourselves into thinking that we know more. Believing that we know our children completely means, inevitably, that we objectify them and do not allow them to take a leading role in their own lives.

Think back again to the Abrams' conversation about Jonny's bar mitzva. David and Sara are concerned about his resistance. They note that he is uncomfortable leading services. Eventually they recognize how much he enjoys helping younger children, and they conclude on a plan for his bar mitzva lessons.

At no point in their conversation do the Abrams reduce Jonny to a label. He does not become shy, energetic, unfocused, or lazy. This is not semantics. It is the difference between observing current behavior and limiting future behavior. Labels limit. Effective parenting means holding open the space (in our own minds) for our children to grow, change, and develop themselves in ways we might never predict or imagine.

THE WORK OF PLAY

The good news is that the approaches we will now explore for "learning" our children are among the most effective antidotes to the fundamental attribution error. The paradigm for most of these approaches is the concept of play.

David Abram and Dan Stein love spending time with their children. Both David and Dan enjoy the special nature of a father-child relationship, and both try to set aside time each weekend to play with their children. But look carefully at how they play:

Dan is in the front yard playing basketball with Adam. Dan was the starting point guard for his own high school team. He's coached Adam's rec league teams for years, and he truly enjoys playing with his son. Either Dan's coaching or his genetics have paid off. Adam made his high school varsity team as a freshman, and he is now the only sophomore in the starting five.

Dan noticed in the last game that Adam favors his right side too heavily. He's picked some drills for his son to improve his left-handed lay-ups. Dan demonstrates the technique, and then Adam practices the drill. When they are done with lay-ups they move on to a shooting drill and Dan shows Adam how to set up properly for a jumper.

Adam enjoys playing with his father, and spending this time together is good for their relationship. But Adam is the only one doing any learning in this situation. Dan may better understand his son's basketball skills at the end of the session, but he is so busy teaching, demonstrating, and critiquing that it is unlikely he will learn much about his son's overall personality and development.

Down the road, the Abrams are also playing basketball in the front yard. But their game looks somewhat different. David played on his high school basketball team, and his son Ben hopes to make the team next year. David helps Ben practice sometimes, but right now they are just playing one-on-one. When Ben was younger, this game was an easy win for David. Now it's more of a competition.

Father and son are both trying hard, but if you watched for a few minutes you would see them both start to laugh. David misses an easy shot, or Ben tries to demonstrate a new move to the basket that winds up with them both on the ground. More importantly, you would see David watching his son play. Not watching him play basketball, but watching him interact, laugh, or focus intensively for a tough play. Ben's basketball skills may or may not improve, but David will have learned more about his son during this time.

Many types of interactions are important for building relationships, but this sort of game, which is about the play itself and not about teaching, improving, or anything else, is a vital component in learning our children.[3]

DIFFERENT WAYS TO PLAY

As adults, we tend to like games with set rules. The more organized the better. Yet when it comes to playing with our children, the less structured the play, the more powerful the opportunity to learn.[4] The parent who allows a six-year-old to invent the scenario and direct the action in their game of pretend will immediately open a window into the child's imagination, dreams, and perception of the world:

---

3. For a striking argument in favor of playing with children by a dedicated Torah scholar, see Rabbi Aharon Lichtenstein, "On Raising Children," http://etzion.org.il/en/raising-children (accessed May 22, 2015).
4. On the importance of play to the child, see Rabbi Shlomo Wolbe, who quotes the famed Rabbi Yisrael Salanter on the intensity of a child's imaginative play as well as its implications for education. See his *Planting and Building: Raising a Jewish Child* (Jerusalem: Feldheim, 1999), 21–23.

Who does the six-year-old dream of becoming?

When she pretends to be a "mommy," how do mommies act?

How does she behave when she is the powerful one in the scenario?

We should not, of course, draw sweeping conclusions from any one interaction. Each one is simply another small slice of our child's personality, and tomorrow's interaction may be very different than today's.

It is easiest for us to see how this sort of obviously imaginative game lets us learn more about our children. It is also easiest for us to allow our children to take the lead in this purely pretend game. We struggle more when it comes to games that are more traditional.

Take Calvinball, the classic non-traditional competitive game made famous by Bill Watterson's *Calvin and Hobbes* comics. Like a typical sport, Calvinball is an intense physical game in which the participants attempt to win at all costs. But unlike a typical sport, the main rule in Calvinball is that you may never play it the same way twice. Rule 1.2, for example, states, "Any player may declare a new rule at any point in the game. The player may do this audibly or silently."[5]

Calvinball itself may be fictional, but the style of play certainly is not. Just play a game of tag, capture the flag, or hide-and-seek with your eight-year-old and you will notice how often the rules change (usually to the eight-year-old's advantage). Watch a group of eight-year-olds play together and you will see them

---

5. For more fun with Calvinball, see any collection of Bill Watterson's *Calvin and Hobbes*, or http://www.picpak.net/calvin/calvinball (accessed December 20, 2015).

negotiate and renegotiate the rules throughout the game.[6] This is true even in more traditional games and sports. No matter how well the official game may have been defined, children will find a point to debate and clarify.

This process quickly infuriates the parent attempting to play with these children. Our instinct is to step in and clarify the rules and avoid the fights that often ensue. Yet what we adults often miss is that the rule-setting itself is part of the play. And so, if we impose our rules rather than let the natural process unfold, we both truncate the play and eliminate the opportunity to learn our children through these interactions.

TEEN PLAY

What is obvious in the case of young children's play is true in a more subtle way in the case of adolescents. For adolescents, much of the "play" comes in choosing the game. Listen to how a group of teenagers discuss, negotiate, and determine what they will do next.

In truth, for adolescents the down time of "hanging out" is play itself. Teenagers will laugh, joke around, and tease one another, all the while exploring how others react to them and figuring their own identity. While our teenagers are unlikely to allow us to participate in a hanging-out session with them and their friends, it is the same mode of "play" that we can replicate in our own interactions with them.

Here too, understandably, parents have a natural tendency to resist:

---

6. For a more in-depth look at children's games and their rules, and an exploration of how boys and girls tend to approach game-related disputes, see Carol Gilligan, *In a Different Voice* (Cambridge: Harvard University Press, 1993).

Adam Stein is relaxing on the couch and playing video games on a Sunday afternoon. Dan has just returned from a morning on call at his practice. There is a long list of things that need to get done around the house. Dan knows that it's not really his son's responsibility to fix the leaky faucet, balance the family bank account, or prepare the taxes. But those items are on Dan's list for the day, and that makes it challenging to avoid feeling some resentment toward his lounging teenage son.

Imagine now what it would take to convince Dan to sit down next to Adam and pick up the other remote control. We know that Dan makes time to coach his son's team, and he makes time to help Adam practice on his own at home too. That sort of involvement with his son feels productive. Playing video games on a Sunday afternoon just seems like a waste of time.

The taxes need to get done, and the faucet needs to get fixed. Yet contrary to Dan's instinctive response, it may be that lounging on the couch with his son for an hour would be more productive than spending that same hour on the basketball court with him.

Why? Because this half-hour on the couch has no set rules or pre-programmed outline. Dan will have the chance to see how Adam sets his parameters, how he teaches a video game to his father (and, most likely, how he behaves when he soundly beats his dad). If Dan lets Adam take the lead, he may learn more about his son in this short period of time than he would in many sessions of teaching him on the court.

Here is where Shabbat and other Jewish holidays can provide one of the most effective supports to our parenting efforts. Shabbat means that we cannot balance our bank accounts, fix the faucet, or cross any of the other to-do items off our list. This simple fact removes one of the barriers to playing effectively with our children.

Between synagogue attendance, extended meals, and play dates, Shabbat is by no means an open-schedule day. However, it is a day when we may be able to step back from our typical to-do list and give ourselves permission to spend what seems to be non-productive time playing with our children.

Shabbat also carries the benefit of limiting our children's, and our own, interaction with electronic entertainment. This, combined with the addition of a certain amount of free time, creates a space particularly suited for the sort of impromptu, imaginative, and interactive play that can truly help us learn our children.

CONVERSATION

Play is a mode that we are not typically used to as adults. In contrast, most parents would say we feel at ease interacting through conversations with our children. Ironically, it is precisely because we assume that we know how to carry on a conversation that we may miss the opportunities that simple dialogues provide to learn our children. Since we do not know what could have been, we often do not even realize what we have missed.

Rachel Stein has just walked in the door from school. Her mom, Debbie, greets her warmly, "How was school, Rach?"

"It was fine, Mom."
"Did anything interesting happen?"
"No. Just a regular day. I'm going to go up to my room."
Later that evening, Dan Stein comes home and Rachel welcomes him, "Hi, Dad."
"Hi Rach. How was your day at school?"
"It was fine."
"Anything you want to tell me?"

"No. Just a regular day. Mom said dinner's going to be ready in a few minutes."

The Steins don't find anything wrong with these exchanges. This represents a typical routine for them. Rachel is in a fine mood, and they will have a nice dinner and a comfortable evening together. If they saw what was unfolding at the Abram house, though, they might have second thoughts.

Ben Abram gets off the school bus and makes his way through the front door. His mom, Sara, is finishing off a chart from the last appointment at her occupational therapy practice. She looks up as Ben walks into the house and greets him warmly, "Hi Ben, welcome home!"

"Hey, Mom, I'm exhausted..."
"What's going on?"
"All my teachers today gave us extra work. I stayed up late last night studying, and now I have two more projects due next week. I'm just overwhelmed with everything right now. Can you give me a hand figuring this out?"

Ben pulls up a chair by his mother and they start to talk it through.

Ben does not come home overwhelmed every night. But whether it's a triumph, a challenge, or just an interesting experience, most evenings he does end up in some form of extended conversation with one of his parents.

FOSTERING COMMUNICATION

The contrast between Rachel's reticence and Ben's communication may be due to their individual natures and tendencies. But it may stem as well from what they have come to expect from their parents' responses.[7]

Which responses will lead our children to share, and which will lead them to demur?

As busy parents, we are often forced to multitask. Debbie Stein is no exception. It is not unusual for her to be finishing up a work conference call while taking Rachel to her soccer game and planning the evening's dinner.

Today at school Rachel had an issue with her friend Jill. Rachel is ready to burst as she sits down in her mom's car. Seeing her mom is still on the phone, Rachel turns on her iPod and starts to play a game of her own.

Every parent has a pickup that goes like this on occasion, but just how often does it happen to the Steins? With one too many experiences feeling that her mom is not fully ready to listen, Rachel becomes less likely to talk.

HOLDING BACK

While a parent's lack of attention leads children to become more reticent, sometimes the problem is just the opposite.

Adam Stein has just returned home from a rough day at his summer job. He's been working the cash register at a local pizza store since school let out, and it has become more and more frustrating. When Adam walks in, his father, Dan, is in the kitchen preparing dinner. Adam sits down and starts his rant:

---

7. For an in-depth discussion of how to enhance parent-child communication, see Adele Faber and Elaine Mazlish, *How to Talk So Kids Will Listen & Listen So Kids Will Talk* (New York: HarperCollins, 2004). Helpful summaries are available online; see http://www.mountvernon.k12.ia.us/uploads/2/6/5/2/26525259/how-to-talk-so-kids-will-listen.pdf (accessed May 25, 2014).

"I can't deal with that guy anymore. Whatever I do is wrong. He doesn't like the way I ring up credit cards. He doesn't like the way I answer the phone."

Dan sees his son is upset and jumps right in to help. "Adam, have you tried talking to him about this? Maybe if you can get him to sit down with you..."

"You don't understand, Dad. He doesn't want to sit down and talk to me. He just wants to criticize everything I do!"

"In that case, what if you wrote him a short note and gave it to him on your way out of work tomorrow?"

"Whatever..."

Dan and Adam both leave this situation feeling frustrated. Dan was trying to be a good, involved father and help his son, yet Adam shoots down any suggestions his dad offers. As outside observers, we know that if this type of exchange repeats itself, Adam will soon be much less likely to share with his father.

AN ALTERNATIVE RESPONSE

What happened here happens in many relationships, but it is a trap to which we are most susceptible as parents. From the time our children are young, we are used to taking care of them, helping them to navigate their surroundings and surmount any obstacles they face.

When Adam turns to his father with this problem, Dan takes the same approach. He wants to help his son. And so he tries to guide Adam toward a solution. The solutions Dan suggests are logical and would likely work. The problem is that Adam is not looking for a solution. He is upset and he is looking for someone to listen.

The irony is that the more we care, the more likely we are to make the same mistake. If we react immediately with questions, suggestions, or solutions to our children's concerns, our children do not feel that their concerns have been heard. They then push back against the proposed solution, causing us to redouble our efforts, as Dan does in this situation.

If instead of solutions we simply give our child an indication that we are listening, the conversation can take a completely different turn. Consider this alternative ending:

...Adam sits down and starts his rant:

"I can't deal with that guy anymore. Whatever I do is wrong. He doesn't like the way I ring up credit cards. He doesn't like the way I answer the phone."
Dan sees his son is upset but resists the urge to jump in. Instead he says, "That is really frustrating."
"Yeah. I don't know what he wants from me."
"That's tough"
"Yeah. I guess I can deal with it, I just don't know why he has to be so rough on me..."

Note that this exchange may or may not result in a solution to Adam's problem. It does result in Adam's feeling heard and supported. This opens the door to Dan's helping with solutions at a point when Adam will be better able to accept them. More important, as a result of this exchange, Adam will be more likely to come to his father with future concerns or frustrations. By restraining his desire to help immediately, Dan opens the door to a deeper relationship in the future.

Restraining our desire to respond immediately increases the likelihood that our children will share more with us in the future. But that is not its only contribution. Pausing first to understand creates the space that allows us to learn our children through these conversations.[8]

WHAT WILL THEY SAY NEXT?

As we saw with the various forms of play, the less directed we make the interaction, the more we can learn about our children. To see this for yourself, try the following experiment. The next time you are in a conversation with your child (or anyone, for that matter), actively try to predict the next sentence before your child says the words.

If you are like most of us, you will notice two things. First, you may be surprised to realize that you were already making this prediction unconsciously. Rather than starting from scratch, you are simply becoming aware of what you were already doing. Second, once you have become conscious of your prediction, you will notice that more often than not it is incorrect.

Why is our guess so often wrong? Simply put, we tend to predict what *we* would say next rather than what the other person would say next.

The danger in our errant predictions is that by the time the other person responds, we have subconsciously colored their words. At times we may even find ourselves responding to what we think they *will* say rather than what they actually said. This does not make for effective conversation in general. It is all the more problematic when it comes to our children.

We have seen that the way our children see the world is shaped and colored by their developmental stage. This means that we are more likely to err in our predictions and more likely

---

8. For a discussion of the advantages of seeking first to understand, then to be understood, across all relationships, see Steven Covey, *The Seven Habits of Highly Effective People* (New York: Simon & Schuster, 1989), Habit 5.

to misunderstand their words. The common complaint "it's not fair," for example, means something completely different when uttered by an eight-year-old and by a twelve-year-old. In both cases, the phrase means something different to the child than it would to an adult.

Pausing before we respond to our children gives us the time to properly understand their words within their developmental context. This enables us to learn more about our children and to respond to what they are actually saying.

With these tools for learning our children in hand, we are ready now to return to the Abram dining room to respond to Ben.

Deeply troubled by what he has learned on Holocaust Remembrance Day, Ben mutters to no one in particular in the middle of dinner, "How could God let that happen? Those people didn't deserve it."

Hearing Ben's comment, the Abrams instinctively place it within a developmental framework. They know that at his age, Ben is struggling to create a cohesive picture of how God relates to the world, and that he is struggling to connect this picture to his sense of self.

After years of playing and talking with Ben, they also know that he needs time to process and mull over ideas. Both Sara and David have learned that Ben does not respond well when they suggest answers to his questions. While they hate to leave a question like this hanging, they know better than to respond right away.

David is sitting next to Ben at the dinner table, and he puts his hand on his son's shoulder. Ben takes another bite of his food, and the dinner conversation moves on.

Later that evening, Ben and Sara are sitting together in the family room. Sara looks at her son and she can tell that he's ready.

"Ben, I don't think any of them deserved it either."

"So why did God let that happen, Mom?"

"I don't know. I am not sure we'll ever know. I struggle with that every year around this time."

"So it doesn't get easier?"

"No, I wouldn't say it gets easier. But I would say that you learn to live with the struggle, and I think I'm a better person for it."

Ben heads off to do his homework. Sara knows that he is still struggling. She also knows that he feels supported and connected to his family, and that those feelings will guide him through this and many more struggles to come.

Part II

Chapter Five

Planting Relationships

Alll of our efforts until now have been devoted to understanding our children. We have seen that children are truly independent individuals at the center of their own lives. We have learned how their cognitive, moral, and faith development affect their understanding of the world at different life stages, and we have explored how we can continue learning our children individually on a nuanced and meaningful level.

As parents, though, we do not merely want to know who our children are, we want to influence who they will become. How do we increase the odds that our children will grow up to embody all the ideals and commitments that we hold dear?

Instinctively, we may assume that the more we want our children to develop a sense of values, the more we must teach and instruct them. This is indeed true, but not always in the way we would think. What we think of as direct teaching is at most half the picture.

Once we appreciate our children's independent existence, nuance, and complexity, we understand that our attempts to help them develop ideals and commitments must be similarly nuanced and complex.

It is no accident that sensitive parents and educators across multiple cultures and centuries have used the image of cultivating a garden to describe the challenges inherent in raising children. The first half of this metaphor focuses on the child as a plant.[1] Indeed, what we have learned about children's self-directed growth and gradually unfolding development resembles the natural processes of a garden where seeds slowly break through their shells, sprout roots, and ultimately blossom.

Now, though, we must shift our focus from the plant to the gardener. What does everything we have learned about children's growth mean for our role as parents? Some clues emerge if we explore how gardening differs from other forms of building.[2]

DIRECT OR INDIRECT EFFORTS?

In most forms of construction, the worker must directly execute any change or improvement necessary in his project. The mason must lay each brick, and the electrician has to connect each wire. In contrast, under the right conditions, the gardener can expect the flower to bloom or the apple to ripen while he is relaxing comfortably at home.

This is how Sara Abram felt about her fifteen-year-old son. She was filled with pride as she watched Ben successfully navigate the challenges of his high school's dual curriculum, athletic

---

1. The image of the child as a plant pervades many cultures. See C. Philip Hwang, Michael E. Lamb, and Irving E. Sigel (eds.), *Images of Childhood* (New York: Psychology Press, 2014). For an application of this metaphor within a Jewish context, see Rabbi Shlomo Wolbe, *Planting and Building* (New York: Feldheim, 1999).
2. Rabbi Wolbe describes a number of differences between a "planting" approach to education and a "building" approach. He advocates a combination of the two approaches for successful child-rearing.

program, and extracurricular activities, all while maintaining a commitment to his family and friends. She would have loved to take the credit for her impressive son, but she could not trace his development to a direct intervention on her part. While people complimented her on her son's character, Sara honestly felt that Ben had blossomed by himself.

But that, of course, is not the whole story. There is another side to the gardener's advantage, a challenge that is illustrated poignantly by an earlier stage in Ben's development.

As a twelve-year-old, Ben Abram was not a particularly organized student. When he arrived home each afternoon, his backpack did not have all the books he needed for his homework (though it did often contain the leftovers from several lunches). When middle school began, Ben and his mom went through a nightly routine of reprimands, followed by phone calls to friends to borrow materials. Yet even once the work was complete, Ben still figured out a way to lose his project before he had a chance to hand it in to the teacher the next day.

Sara worked with her son. She bought him a new agenda in which he could list his assignments and a binder where he could store them, and she reminded him to use these daily. There were even (too many) times that she sat and did his homework with him just to ensure that he would complete it. But despite all of Sara's efforts, Ben's seventh-grade habits did not change. He forgot his homework just as many times in May as he had in September.

THE GARDENER'S QUANDARY

The gardener enjoys how the flowers bloom without direct intervention, but he also knows that if the plants struggle to grow he cannot simply step in and save them. The plumber can grab a wrench and tighten the pipe. The gardener has no tool for forcing a flower to blossom. Such was Sara's dilemma with Ben. There was no way for her to directly intervene to alter the organizational skills of her twelve-year-old.

This is the gardener's quandary: What do you do if your flowers will not bloom?

Direct intervention is not an option. But that does not mean the gardener is helpless. A talented grower faced with struggling plants knows that the solution lies somewhere in the surrounding environment. The plants may be getting too little sunlight or insufficient rain. The soil may not have enough nutrients, or there may be too many surrounding plants competing for nourishment. The gardener's task is to identify and remedy the environmental deficiency.

Sara Abram's direct intervention with twelve-year-old Ben was not getting her anywhere. Each afternoon was filled with nagging reminders and fights with her son. Neither of them was happy, and the routine showed no signs of changing. Then Sara started to broaden her thinking. Was there anything else she could do to help her son?

Talking with Ben, it struck Sara that he had about five minutes from when he got out of his last class until the school bus left. In that time he had to remember his assignments, pack his bag, and get down the stairs and into the bus line. Thinking about how long it took Ben just to get his sneakers on each morning at home, she knew that making it from his last class to the school bus must be a significant challenge.

Sara delved more into the rhythms of Ben's day. She began to ask him how much time he had between classes to hand in his homework, get to his locker, and exchange his books and materials (three minutes), and how often he was late to class (more often than not).

Now Sara saw a different picture. Rather than a disorganized, frustrating kid, she began to see a boy who was having trouble keeping up with the pace of his environment. As he struggled to make it to the bus on time, it was no wonder that Ben forgot half his assignments. It was shocking that he even remembered his backpack! And as he was constantly worried about getting his materials and making it to the next class, it was no surprise that Ben either forgot to bring his completed assignments with him or forgot to hand them in.

THE ENVIRONMENT

As a careful gardener, Sara set to work adjusting Ben's environment. First, she was able to arrange a carpool home from school in place of the bus. The parents driving carpool knew that Ben needed a few extra minutes to gather his things, and Ben knew that he was not going to miss his ride. Though it was only a difference of a few minutes, this small change had a major impact on Ben's stress level. He found he was suddenly able to concentrate when it came time to pack up his things.

Sara did not have the ability to change the class schedule at school, but she knew that its rhythm was also hindering Ben's success. She worked with Ben's principal to identify a number of adjustments that would ease the time pressure within Ben's day. Between some teachers allowing Ben out of class a moment early and others giving him permission to arrive a minute late, Ben's transition time became much more manageable for him.

Sara cannot fix Ben's organizational skills directly. Yet by pruning Ben's environment she opens the space for him to grow. The ways in which we prune may vary depending on the specific child and situation, but we must always note the fundamental difference between Sara's initial unsuccessful attempts and her later efforts.

At first, Sara's focus was on adjustments that Ben himself would need to implement, such as an agenda or a binder. These are direct interventions that aim to change a child's behavior, and they often fail because they are undercut by the very lack of organization they are meant to remedy. Sara's later interventions required nothing additional of Ben himself. She did not ask him to get his things together quickly. Rather, she created extra time and reduced the pressure and anxiety surrounding key transitions in Ben's day.

Indirect interventions rarely produce immediate results, just as plucking the weeds does not immediately make the flowers bloom. But in the long term, Sara's work truly enabled Ben to grow.

RELATIONSHIPS

Indirect interventions are often necessary, but they are not, in fact, the most important part of the growing process. Perhaps the single most important factor in promoting healthy growth is the parent-child relationship. This relationship underlies, supports, and colors the entire education and development process.

Though psychologists debate the precise nature of its influence, they widely agree that the parent-child relationship determines how children learn, explore the world, and establish their own life structures as they grow.[3] In this vein, it is self-evident that children growing up with loving caregivers are more likely to develop healthy patterns and make positive life choices.

But here we need to look a bit deeper. After all, we know that both the Abram and the Stein children are blessed with parents who care for them lovingly. Yet the nuances of the relationships in the two families differ in important ways. These differences shed light on how some approaches to the parent-child relationship are more likely to foster the kind of growth we want.

---

3. The study of how parent-child relationships affect future development is often termed attachment theory. For a foundational work in this field, see Mary Ainsworth et al., *Patterns of Attachment* (Hillsdale, N.J.: Erlbaum, 1978).

PLAY REVISITED

Let's go back to the way we saw Dr. Stein and Mr. Abram playing with their children in the previous chapter.

Dan Stein is in the front yard teaching Adam to improve his left-handed lay-ups. It's wonderful that the two of them are spending time together, and Dan is doing a great job teaching new basketball skills to his son.

When we last analyzed this situation, we noted that Dan is so busy teaching that he may not learn much about his son. If we move beyond this specific point to examine the relationship itself, we will see a similarly one-sided development process.

The nature of their play together means that Dan is in charge and instructs Adam. Adam may respond dutifully, but his role is reactive only. This effectively limits the bandwidth across which their bond develops. Interactions in which Dan is directly instructing Adam are important, but they will only develop the relationship along the uneven playing field of a teacher-student dynamic.

Parents have much to teach their children. And some of this teaching should happen in the form of direct instruction. However, we must be sensitive to the limits of such instruction in facilitating holistic growth, and we must be aware that too much instruction can create tension and rebellion within the parent-child relationship.

A VARIETY OF INTERACTIONS

Down the block, the Abrams are also playing basketball in the front yard. Rather than practicing specific drills, they are playing a game of one-on-one, with the competition occasionally punctuated by a silly joke or moment of conversation.

We noted earlier that this sort of play enables David Abram to learn more about his son, Ben. Looking at this interaction from a relationship lens, we see that Ben and David are playing together on an even field. Ben's role is just as active as David's, and the exchanges proceed along multiple valences at the same time. Ben is alternatively joking, serious, or playful *because* David allows him the space to initiate these varied types of exchanges.

Why are such varied exchanges important?

Think about the relationship you have with a co-worker whom you see only at the office. This is a person you have worked with for years, whose personal life you have learned about during coffee breaks, and whose spouse you have met at the company picnic. Yet if asked to describe your relationship, you will most likely refer to this person as a co-worker or colleague rather than as a friend. Your relationship is defined by the boundaries of the office, which limit the range and depth of your connection.

While we tend to think of relationships as abstract entities, they are, in fact, founded on a series of concrete interactions. Relationships built only on a few types of interaction tend to be narrowly bounded, while those built through a wider variety of experiences have greater depth and resilience.

In fact, the realization that relationships are neither a matter of biology nor an abstract concept may itself be the most crucial first step. As parents, we often assume that our relationships with our children began the day they were born. Our own identities are shaped by the fact that we are mothers and fathers, and our children's identities are shaped as sons or daughters.

The fact that we identify as mothers and fathers, however, does not automatically translate into a relationship with our children. We become parents when our children are born, and we remain their parents (as we often like to remind them) even when they are grown. But relationships with our children must be built consciously and continuously through interactions spanning years and decades.

QUALITY TIME

The way we choose to spend time with our children over these years and decades will determine the nature of our relationship. New research suggests, in fact, that the amount of time we spend with our children is less important than the quality of the time we spend with them.[4]

Quality time is not easily planned.[5] Researchers have identified family dinners, collaborating on homework, and family vacations as key opportunities for relationship-building. But any parent can tell you that sometimes the best quality time comes in unexpected ways – while stuck in line at a grocery store, for instance, or in a traffic jam – and that some family dinners or vacations can go quite awry.

How, then, do we maximize the quality time we have with our children?

Here we return to the basic foundation we laid in the opening chapter. Our ability to turn time into quality time and to use daily interactions to build our relationships depends on how we view our children. We learned earlier that putting our children at the center means seeing them as independent individuals who

---

4. Melissa A. Milkie, Kei Nomaguchi, and Kathleen Denny, "Does the Amount of Time Mothers Spend with Children or Adolescents Matter?"*Journal of Marriage and Family* 77 (2015): 355–72. It is important to note that the key outcomes studied in this article, such as the likelihood of children's making healthy choices, avoiding at-risk behavior, and pursuing academic achievement, would be necessary but not sufficient in our view of what we want for our children.

See also the popular media reaction to this study, including the following: http://www.wsj.com/articles/the-right-way-to-do-family-time-1428076067 and http://www.washingtonpost.com/local/making-time-for-kids-study-says-quality-trumps-quantity/2015/03/28/10813192-d378-11e4-8fce-3941fc548f1c_story.html (both accessed June 18, 2015).

5. See, for example, the Motherload blog, http://parenting.blogs.nytimes.com/2015/03/31/quantity-time-begets-quality-time-and-parents-spend-enough-of-both/?_r=0 (accessed June 18, 2015).

are the subjects of their own lives. Translating this into daily inter-actions, however, can be more challenging than it seems.

It's a Sunday morning and Debbie Stein is about to set out on a day of errands. The holidays are coming up soon, Rachel's soccer season is starting, and this is the last available Sunday for the next few weeks. In order for Debbie to get Rachel her new cleats and still make it to the other stores, Rachel will need to accompany her mom on the day's errands.

As they start out on their errands, Rachel asks if they can go to the athletic store first. She's excited about getting her new cleats. This is not the order Debbie had in mind, and it makes the driving route less convenient.

Later, in the supermarket, Rachel asks if she can choose the snacks for the week. She promises not to buy anything more than her mom usually purchases, but Debbie knows that Rachel will take twice as long to make her choices.

Finally, on their way home, Rachel asks if they can drive by her friend's home so she can quickly show off her new soccer gear. It's only down the block, but by this time, Debbie is worn out from the day of shopping and itching to get home.

None of Rachel's requests is objectively important, certainly from an adult perspective, and no parent should be expected to say yes to all of a child's requests.

How she chooses to respond, though, will reveal whether Debbie sees her daughter as an independent individual accompa-nying her or as a mere tag-along for the day. Will Debbie acknowl-edge the validity of Rachel's desires, though they may not be important from an adult perspective, or will she simply brush off her daughter's requests as distractions from the important tasks of the day?

Debbie may be most likely to respond positively to Rachel's final request, since at that point the errands are finally done. Yet it may be the response to Rachel's first request that is most important, since that exchange can make the difference between mother and daughter setting out for a day of errands or a day of unplanned quality time.

HOME-BASE

This sort of quality time is crucial for establishing the kind of relationship that psychologists have identified as the foundation for healthy development. How so?

Back when Lisa Abram was two years old, she and her father David walked into the nursery school playroom for the first time. They sat down together on one of the couches set up for caregivers. Within a few minutes, Lisa became curious. She set out to explore the block-building corner, which was closest to the couch. After a few minutes of play, Lisa grabbed one of the blocks and retreated back to the couch to sit with her father. A moment later, she was off again, this time venturing across the room to the toy trucks for some time before once again returning to David's lap.

This back-and-forth pattern may seem frustrating to the uninitiated caregiver. Why won't Lisa just engage in one of the play areas consistently? But to the psychologist, this is precisely the pattern of healthy development. The parent provides a safe-space, where the child feels secure and comfortable. From this base, the child can set out to find her way, taking small risks each time as she explores further and further, and then returning to her home-base.

This phenomenon of toddler development is reiterated again in the teenage years, with the concrete, physical patterns of safety and exploration being acted out in a broader orbit. As teenagers search out their own identities, they too will explore through new social groups, behaviors, and experiences. Teens who have strong relationships with their parents will be more likely to engage in this exploration in a safe manner, returning from each excursion to revisit their home-base. This time, though, the excursions may last days or months, and the home-base is not the parent's lap but rather the parent's values.

TOO CONNECTED?

This developmental pattern emphasizes the need for connection. Yet it also highlights the need for exploration opportunities. Imagine that instead of sitting on the couch, David Abram accompanied Lisa to the block corner, and then to the trucks, and so on. It would be wonderful for father and daughter to play together. But if taken to the extreme, Lisa's growth would be inhibited, because she would never learn to explore safely.

This danger, too, exists in teenage development. While they continue to provide a safe-base, parents must consciously allow their children to visit the teenage equivalent of the block-corner. This does not mean allowing our teenagers to engage in risk-taking behavior, but it does mean allowing them space within the relationship to encounter and explore challenges on their own. If we do not do so, even the most well-meaning parents can stunt their own children's growth.[6]

It's 10:30 a.m. and Debbie Stein glances at her phone. She has just received her fourth text message from her twelve-year-old daughter. Rachel is melting down in school after receiving a poor grade on her English project, followed by a lunch detention for having let the teacher know just how unfair he was.

Debbie has been trying to ignore the multiple texts, but she doesn't particularly like this English teacher. Rachel's report

---

6. "Helicopter-parenting" is a term coined relatively recently by researchers. While the full picture is still just emerging, most studies point to the negative effects of this approach to child-rearing. See, for example, http://web.sbs.arizona.edu/college/news/dangers-overparenting (accessed June 23, 2015) and Patricia Somers and Jim Settle, "The Helicopter Parent: Research Toward a Typology," *College and University* 86, no.1 (2010).

of the lunch detention puts Debbie over the edge. Within a few moments, Debbie has stepped out of her work meeting and is on the phone with Rachel's principal, explaining Rachel's side of the story. Either because he is convinced, or because Debbie is a past PTA chair, the principal eventually agrees to intervene. Rachel's grade stays the same, but she is excused from her lunch detention.

By the strict measure of justice, Rachel may or may not have deserved a detention. Regardless, though, her mother's intervention has robbed Rachel of a key opportunity to develop her own ability to cope with the typical stressors and challenges of everyday life. Learning to manage through such situations is, in fact, a key factor in children's future success, and a classic arena in which parents must allow their children to explore.[7]

Most parents now communicate with their children through digital or social media. On the one hand, this is a positive development. If our children are comfortable in this mode of communication, if it is how children often "speak" to their friends, then we as parents should engage with them in their native language.

Yet we must be aware of the dangers inherent in this mode of communication. Even if Debbie had not reacted by calling the principal to intervene, Rachel's immediate outlet of texting her mother means that she may not learn to cope with her frustrations by developing emotional self-management skills.

The constant availability of a parental ear, even when the child is in the midst of school, camp, or another valuable experience, can in and of itself impede healthy child development. This availability means that the child never truly leaves the parent's lap

---

7. For a cogent argument on the value of allowing our children to encounter such challenges, see Paul Tough, *How Children Succeed: Grit, Curiosity, and the Hidden Power of Character* (New York: Houghton Mifflin Harcourt, 2013).

in order to explore and encounter the challenges of daily life as an independent individual.

THE RIGHT RELATIONSHIP

To be clear, it is not only a child's over-communication with the parent that can impede development. The hyperconnectivity allowed by digital media exacerbates the potential for inappropriate communication from parent to child as well.

If Debbie Stein is quick to react to her daughter's texts, she may also be quick to dash off a text of her own. Fifteen-year-old Adam may have forgotten to take the garbage out (again) on his way to school this morning, Rachel may have left her clothing all over her room, or Debbie may just want to share something about her own day with one of her children.

The danger in any of these interchanges is that Debbie is unlikely to be conscious of the parent-child relationship as she communicates in a quick text message. We would be shocked to hear any of the following in person, yet we would not be all that surprised to find them on an iPhone:

> *Rachel:* Sarah is being such a witch again. I hate her.
> *Mom:* Ignore her. She's mean just like her mother.
> *Adam:* I'm going to Jason's after school, ok?
> *Dad:* Just don't be home late. You know how your mom gets if dinner's late. She's in a mood today.
> *Rachel:* Mrs. B. just gave me a detention again. I didn't do anything.
> *Dad:* Sorry, honey. My boss is being a jerk today too. Must be something in the water.

At first, this concern may seem counterintuitive. We have suggested that more opportunities for parents and children to play, to communicate, and to spend time together enhance their relationship. So why would we be concerned about too much quick communication?

We saw earlier that parents who are always busy instructing their children, like Dr. Stein playing basketball with Adam, do a disservice to their relationship-building efforts. Yet while we should not always be instructing our children, we *must* always be aware that they are learning from us through our relationship.

The need to build a relationship with our children should not mislead us to confuse this relationship with any other friendship or connection in our lives. Our relationship must be both broad and deep, but if we want to guide and support our children, we must consciously shape it as a parent-child relationship.

Over-sharing is dangerous. We must be aware that what we choose to communicate with our children informs their perception both of us and of our relationship. Snarky and negative comments devalue our relationships, and when those comments refer to our spouse or children they are all the more damaging.

Even if our over-sharing is not negative, these comments can skew the appropriate balance of our relationship with our children. The parent-child relationship includes a responsibility to set appropriate boundaries for the child's behavior that would be inappropriate in any other friendship or family relationship. We will revisit the topic of discipline later, but for now, understanding the need for both love and limits with our children highlights the unique nature of this relationship.[8]

One of the best guides to crafting this relationship comes in the form of the mitzva of honoring our parents. We typically

---

8. For an interesting work on this topic, see Raphael Pelcovitz and David Pelcovitz, *Balanced Parenting: A Father and a Son – a Rabbi and a Psychologist – Examine Love and Limits in Raising Children* (New York: Artscroll Mesorah, 2005).

think of this area of Jewish practice as a series of obligations incumbent on the child: not contradicting a parent or not sitting in a parent's chair, on the one hand, and caring for parents' basic needs, on the other.

A more helpful understanding for our parenting efforts would be to see this series of laws as the framework for an effective relationship, infused with warmth and caring, and at the same time always cognizant of the education and growth that the relationship must support.[9] It is only on the foundation of such a relationship that we can meaningfully explore any of the educational approaches in the coming chapters.

---

9. In his classes at Yeshiva University (1996), Rabbi Aharon Kahn argued that this understanding is evident in Maimonides' portrayal of the laws relating to the respect owed both to parents and to Torah teachers.

Chapter Six

Meaningful Models

We have seen Adam Stein sitting in synagogue on Saturday morning. He arrives on time with his father, but he most certainly does not look happy to be there. We have already noted that the main synagogue service may not be an age-appropriate expectation for Adam. But what other factors contribute to Adam's behavior?

We have watched Rachel Stein's disappointing social behavior at her bat mitzva. We explained that Rachel's behavior may be connected to her stage of moral development, and to possible missteps in the logic her parents used in their attempt to guide her toward more empathic behavior. Here too, though, it is a good bet that further examination will reveal other factors contributing to Rachel's behavior.

Before we re-examine these episodes, let's take a broader look at how parents shape their children's lives.

ACCENTS AND ATTITUDES

If you want to examine the impact of one generation on the next, the United States is a great place to look. After all, the United States is a country populated almost entirely by immigrants. In the early days of the Republic, settlers arrived mostly in regional groups, transplanted from their native lands to a new social, geographical, and national context. As they raised children and grandchildren in the new setting, many attempted to transmit their belief system and values to the next generation.

Yet that is not all that parents passed on to their children. In a groundbreaking book, the historian David Hackett Fischer identifies the complex and multifaceted way that early settlers influenced Americans through today.[1] Fischer shows that in each generation, children inherited not only what their parents passed on intentionally, like systems of values and religion, but also behaviors that their parents transmitted unintentionally, such as eating patterns, dress, and social relationships.

To take a benign example, think for a moment about the various accents you encounter in different geographical regions of the United States. What passes for an *o* in one part of the country is an *a* in another, in some places *r*'s are added where none should be (fellow – *feller*), and speakers in other places can't seem to hold on to the *r*'s they do have (drawer – *draw*, art – *aht*). These patterns of speech are not new or random. They fairly faithfully represent the patterns that the original settlers in each of these regions brought from their native England, Scotland, or Ireland, and they have been passed down from parent to child for the last two hundred years.

How have accents survived the generations?

---

1. David Hackett Fischer, *Albion's Seed: Four British Folkways in America* (Oxford: Oxford University Press, 1989).

Picture some parent in South Carolina sitting her three-year-old down in the living room: "OK, Jimmy, remember when you want to speak to someone we don't say 'you,' we say 'y'all.'" The image is clearly absurd. Children do not learn accents through direct instruction. Rather, they naturally imitate their parents' cadence and pronunciation until they too develop similar patterns of speech.[2]

This pattern is so natural that it is sometimes called social inheritance. The phenomenon of modeling and imitation explains how early settlers passed the full array of their culture to their children. It also explains a great deal of how we influence and impact our own children.[3]

SOCIAL INHERITANCE

We constantly model a full array of behavioral patterns for our children. Yet just as we do not hear our own accents, we rarely see these other behavioral patterns in ourselves. As a result, we often influence our children in ways that we ourselves do not even recognize.[4]

---

2. Of course, it is not just parents who serve as role models. We are constantly surrounded by models of everything, from speech to dress and behavior. This is evident to anyone who has seen the child of new immigrants learn the native accent from classmates instead of parents. In this chapter we focus on the specific impact of the parent as role model. We will return to the potential effects of peers.

3. The most powerful description of the psychology of the power of role-modeling in child development is provided by Albert Bandura, *Social Learning Theory* (Englewood Cliffs, N.J.: Prentice Hall, 1977).

4. Bandura explains that children imitate a variety of behaviors that they see in various role models. However, children are predisposed not only to imitate their parents but also to identify with them. Identification means that the child will not just mimic specific behaviors but also adopt the parents' values, beliefs, and attitudes.
On the power of other adults, and educators in particular, who may serve as role models for children, see http://www.infed.org/informaljewisheducation/informal_jewish_education.htm (accessed July 1, 2015).

Turn back now to Adam Stein, sitting bored in synagogue. Obviously on one level his father, Dan, believes that synagogue attendance is important. Dan is exhausted from the work week, and he could certainly use a bit more sleep, but he is up early every Shabbat morning. Rain or shine he is in synagogue from start to finish.

It would be safe to say that Dan models a commitment to synagogue attendance. And, for his part, Adam has imitated this commitment as he joins his father each week.

But what else may Dan be modeling along the way?

If we look closer, we may find that something is lacking during Dan's time in the synagogue. Dan is in synagogue, but how is he participating in prayers? Is he reading the words of the prayers reluctantly, or not at all? Does he maintain a positive affect that masks his inner boredom while he waits for the opportunity to socialize at the end of (or during) prayers?

Alternatively, the hidden challenge may come before Dan enters the synagogue. As he readies himself to leave his home each Shabbat morning, what is Dan's attitude? Is he heading out the door with a smile, or would he rather spend a few more minutes relaxing with his cup of coffee?

Assume for a moment that Dan falls out on the lesser side of any of these questions. He is acting appropriately and demonstrating commitment, but his inner state may not be aligned with this external demonstration. As far as his own mitzva performance is concerned, we may be willing to give Dan a pass. After all, the Talmud often tells us that doing a mitzva for the wrong reason is praiseworthy, as it will ultimately lead us to fulfill it for the right reason.[5]

---

5. See, for example, Sanhedrin 105b.

Yet as far as Dan's children are concerned, this is a dangerous duality. Adam's scowl in synagogue simply reveals what is behind the mask of Dan's socially acceptable smile. This is the painful truth of what it means to serve as a role model. Our children do not just imitate what we say. They are much more attuned to the accent and cadence beneath the words. This danger may, in fact, be what lies behind the talmudic dictum, "Any scholar whose inside is not like his outside is no scholar."[6]

SURFACE VALUES AND DEEP VALUES

To understand the educational equivalent of the accents we pass on to our children, it is helpful to differentiate between what we can term "surface values" and "deep values." Surface values are beliefs and commitments that we verbalize, and even adhere to in practice, but do not penetrate to the core of our lives. Deep values, in contrast, are values and beliefs that fundamentally shape how we see the world.

The best way to understand what we mean by deep values is to think back to the description of children's developmental stages in Chapter 3. The psychologists Piaget, Kohlberg, and Fowler each define developmental stages in slightly different terms. However, common to all three is that the perspective of each developmental stage is the lens that determines how children see everything in their world.

On this point, Fowler is particularly helpful. He identifies "faith" as that with which a person is ultimately concerned at any given stage. This "ultimate concern" is the equivalent of what we have termed deep values. Our deep values underlie our actions and decision-making processes. It is primarily these values that our children naturally imitate.

---

6. Yoma 72b.

Deep values are broad beliefs that influence significant life-choices, but if we revisit Rachel Stein's bat mitzva, we can see at least a snapshot of their power. Recall that the Steins were very disappointed with Rachel's behavior. Despite her speech and project about acting kindly toward others, Rachel showed that her primary concerns revolved around her own social standing. She insensitively excluded many of her classmates at her own party.

The Steins have encouraged Rachel to be kind to her friends. They insisted that she focus her learning on the topic, and that she invite her entire class (not just her close friends) to her party. Yet Debbie Stein's conversation with the caterer may reveal a slice of her own deep values in this area:

> *Debbie:* And let's make sure we don't have that pasta salad that the Silvers served last month. I don't know what they were thinking with that.
> *Caterer:* No problem, Debbie. Just let me know what you want instead.
> *Debbie:* Great. Let's do something that you have not done for other bat mitzvas. I want this one to be special. Can you put together a new menu for me?
> *Caterer:* Sure. Anything else?
> *Debbie:* Let's also talk about the decor. Can you do something new with the linens and centerpieces? If you can't handle that, I can get a party planner to come up with something.

There is nothing wrong with wanting your child's bat mitzva to be beautiful, exciting, and special. But what are the deep values that guide Debbie's actions?

Is it a desire to celebrate Rachel's growth, to come together with family and rejoice in the mitzva? Or, alternatively, is Debbie motivated more by a desire to impress her friends and solidify her own social standing in the community?

If the latter is true, the deep values of social standing will impact Rachel more deeply than the verbally expressed concern for kindness. To be clear, it does not matter whether Rachel overhears this particular conversation with the caterer. Whether it is overhearing another conversation that Dan and Debbie have about the invitation list, watching her mother prepare the seating arrangements, or any of the other myriad interactions surrounding their social lives, Debbie's deep values will become clear to her daughter.

So what is Debbie to do?

HEAL THYSELF

Until now we have focused primarily on how we see and relate to our children. When it comes to role modeling, though, we must turn the focus squarely on ourselves. Effective modeling begins with a careful examination of our commitments and an honest appraisal of our deep values.

The good news is that being a parent is a wonderful motivator and guide for self-improvement. First, as motivation, our desire to guide and support our children gives a new level of importance to our choices. Second, as guidance, our children's behavior can often serve as a mirror to highlight areas in which we ourselves may be falling short.

After the bat mitzva, Debbie and Dan are frustrated with Rachel. Their reaction is quite understandable, especially given the emotions surrounding a family celebration. They most certainly should speak to Rachel about her behavior (in a way that she can understand at her developmental stage).

What Debbie and Dan must also do, and this is more challenging, is turn the focus back on their own behaviors. This episode gives the Steins the opportunity to ask themselves whether they are inadvertently modeling values that contribute to Rachel's negative behavior.

These are difficult questions to ask ourselves as parents. We are most pained to see our children fall short in those areas that we know pose a challenge for us as well. Our natural tendency is to express this pain as anger or disappointment in our children. But in truth, both we and our children are better served if we allow these experiences to shine a light on our own deep values.

MODELING EMOTIONS

Through the middle of the twentieth century, Jewish immigrants to Manhattan's Lower East Side did not have it easy. They arrived penniless, or close to it, and began searching for work. At the time, the Lower East Side was a center of garment manufacturing (the so-called *shmatta* business), and this became the primary source of employment for the majority of immigrants.

Yet this was a time before labor regulations required safe working conditions or a limit on the hours a worker could be made to labor in a day or a week. Immigrants working in sweatshops were required to work at least six, if not seven, days a week. Of course, anti-discrimination laws in employment would not be enacted for decades.

The observant Eastern European Jewish immigrant was left in a precarious state. If he was willing to work Saturdays, he could find relatively steady work. Many immigrants, fearing for their family's sustenance, chose this path.

Others refused to violate the Sabbath no matter the cost. These immigrants followed a storied routine of searching for work each Monday morning, knowing that come Friday afternoon they would be fired for leaving early, and would need to start a new job search the next Monday. The dedication that these immigrants displayed toward their Sabbath observance was legendary.

Given the dedication of these parents, it was a surprise to the community that many of their children did not themselves choose to remain Sabbath-observant. This was all the more surprising given that such observance had become much easier for the children's generation, so many of whom were doctors or lawyers or involved in other white-collar occupations where Saturday work was not required.

Much can be said about the general forces of assimilation at play for this second generation, and undoubtedly these significantly influenced the children's choice of lifestyle. However, there is another factor to consider as we reflect on the parent as role model.

SHVER TZU ZEIN A YID

In an oft-repeated story, it is said that this concern was brought to the leading rabbinic figure of that generation, Rabbi Moshe Feinstein, himself an immigrant to Manhattan's Lower East Side. How, Rav Moshe's students asked him, can the children of such dedicated parents leave their family's values behind?

Rabbi Feinstein answered by adding one detail to the story we recounted above. The dedicated Jewish immigrant finds new work each Monday. He works five days of taxing labor in the sweatshop, only to be fired on Friday afternoon. Returning to his small apartment to prepare for the Sabbath, he groans in Yiddish, "*Oy, es iz shver tzu zein a Yid* – It is difficult to be a Jew."

Without denigrating the commitment of the father, Rabbi Feinstein asked, "Why would children who hear this refrain choose to pursue the lifestyle that caused their father such pain?"

One cannot reduce the assimilation of a generation to a single factor. Yet for our purposes, Rabbi Feinstein's question highlights a striking new aspect of role modeling. We have seen that parents model everything from external behaviors to deep values. But beyond all of this, parents model an emotional attitude towards their commitments, which can be most influential of all.[7]

This, then, exposes an additional danger in Dan's attitude toward shul attendance. If he is, in fact, reluctant to leave his cup of coffee each Saturday morning, and if Dan acts or speaks in a way that reveals this reluctance to Adam, what he is actually modeling for his son is a begrudging commitment to synagogue attendance.

Faced with the model of a reluctant synagogue-goer, we must wonder what Adam himself will decide when he chooses his own path. We must also consider whether Dan's educational efforts would be better served by happily going late to prayers rather than begrudgingly arriving on time. (Ideally, of course, Dan will respond to Adam's scowl not by admonishing his son but instead by re-examining how his own attitudes may be impacting his children.)

What is true of Dan's attitude toward synagogue is perhaps too often true of our attitude toward other mitzvot. Understanding this forces us to ask ourselves difficult questions:

Do we spend hours preparing for Passover but complain bitterly about the work?

Do we punctiliously observe a three-day festival but gripe about its length?

Do we make substantial sacrifices to provide our children a Jewish education but grumble about the cost or quality of their schooling?

Answering these kinds of questions honestly will force most of us to re-examine the attitude we are modeling for our children.

---

7. Albert Bandura, in *Social Learning Theory*, explores various factors that can influence a child's tendency to imitate modeled behavior. One such factor, "vicarious reinforcement," explains that witnessing a model suffer the negative consequences of a chosen behavior makes the child less likely to imitate that behavior. In this way, immigrants who modeled the pain of Shabbat observance made it less likely that their children would adopt the behavior that led to the pain.

BRINGING IT TOGETHER

We have seen that both relationship building and role modeling are powerful forces in shaping our children's growth. Watch what happens when we bring these two forces together.

Most of us have had this awkward experience in the grocery store. We have completed our shopping and are on line at the checkout. Behind us in line are a father and his two sons. By the looks of their cart, they have been in the store for a while and the kids are starting to jostle each other.

Soon the older one gets upset and starts yelling at his younger brother. Seeing the commotion, the frazzled dad turns to his son and growls, "Stop it! Don't you dare yell at your brother! We don't handle things in this family by yelling. He's little and you need to be patient with him!"

Watching the episode, you feel a mix of empathy and embarrassment. The irony here is evident to everyone except dad himself: he is yelling at his son not to yell and demonstrating a lack of patience as he admonishes his son to be calm.

The children, realizing that they have made their father angry, will stop their current behavior out of fear or obedience. But what will they have learned long-term? They have heard the content of their father's words, "do not yell" and "be patient," but his words are overshadowed by his actions. In fact, dad has just shown them that when you are out of patience, the best way to quickly get what you want is to yell. And it is this behavior that they are most likely to adopt for themselves.[8]

This is the paradox of the discipline process. A vital part of our role as parents is to provide boundaries, limits, and guidance

---

8. For a broader discussion of this phenomenon, see Albert Bandura, Dorothea Ross, and Sheila A. Ross, "Transmission of Aggression Through the Imitation of Aggressive Models," *Journal of Abnormal and Social Psychology* 63 (1961): 575–58.

for our children. However, discipline colored by anger and impatience teaches anger and impatience. Such discipline generates short-term gains in compliance at the expense of long-term damage to the child's healthy development.

MODELING RELATIONSHIPS

What should concern us most about this example is that the father is not merely modeling a behavior for his children. He is also modeling an approach to family relationships. All parents lose patience with their children on occasion, especially when stuck in a long checkout line. But if this kind of reaction occurs with some frequency, it will begin to color the parent-child relationship.

The damage this causes is twofold. First, as we learned in the previous chapter, the parent-child relationship is the bridge that allows us to guide our children's growth and development. Second, the parent-child relationship colors how our children perceive us as role models.[9]

Children are naturally predisposed to identify with their parents. Identification leads to imitation, not just of specific behaviors but of beliefs, values, and attitudes. But if the parent-child relationship is colored by anger or frustration, the identification process can be fundamentally undermined.

At the most extreme, this may lead the child to fully reject the parents' value system. In more routine cases, it subtly weakens the child's desire to follow in the parents' footsteps. While this effect is often almost imperceptible at first, many adults trace their value choices directly back to their relationships with their parents and, by extension, with their parents' value systems.

---

9. See n 4 above.

MODELING FOR GOD

When it comes to religious values, the connection between relationships and modeling encompasses yet another dimension. Consider the following series of talmudic teachings:

> Our Rabbis taught: It is said: "Honor thy father and thy mother"; and it is also said: "Honor the Lord with thy substance": thus the Torah compares the honor due to parents to that of God.
>
> It is said: "Ye shall fear every man his father and his mother"; and it is also said: "The Lord thy God thou shalt fear, and Him thou shalt serve": thus the Torah compares the fear of parents to the fear of God.
>
> It is said: "And he that curses his father, or his mother, shall surely be put to death"; and it is also said: "Whosoever curses his God shall bear his sin": thus the Bible compares the blessing (cursing) of parents to that of God.
>
> When a man honors his father and his mother, the Holy One, blessed be He, says: "I ascribe [merit] to them as though I had dwelt among them and they had honored Me."
>
> When a man vexes his father and his mother, the Holy One, blessed be He, says: "I did right in not dwelling among them, for had I dwelt among them, they would have vexed Me."[10]

When we first read these teachings, we tend to see them from the perspective of the child upon whom this duty rests. By equating the honor due parents to that due God, the Talmud impresses

---

10. Kiddushin 30b and 31a, translation from Soncino Edition with stylistic adjustments by author.

upon children the importance of honoring their parents. For this mitzva the stakes are doubled: respecting parents is not simply an interpersonal obligation, it is a spiritual requirement as well.

Now read the teachings again, but this time from the perspective of the parent. The Talmud highlights the connection between the child's relationship to the parent and the child's relationship to God. What must parents learn from this equation?

Interspersed among the comparisons noted above is the following explanation: "And this is but logical, since...our Rabbis taught: There are three partners in man, the Holy One, blessed be He, the father, and the mother."

Parents are God's partners in the creation of a child. The corollary: Parents must understand that they themselves are the closest concrete representation of God that their child will ever encounter.

This does not mean that parents have supernatural powers. It does mean that children will naturally pattern their relationships with God after their relationships with their parents. To paraphrase the Talmud, children who want to make their parents proud will want to make God proud, and children who feel love from their parents will feel love from God. The reverse, of course, is also true.

We saw how Dan Stein's attitude toward prayer, a key component in his connection to God, shapes his son Adam's prayer. But now a layer has been added. As parents, we can expect our children to model their relationships with God after our relationship with God. But even more, we can expect our children to model their relationships with God after their relationships with us.

(IN)CONSISTENCY

We are models for our children through what we do, through what we believe, and through the relationships we create. If that is not sufficiently intimidating, we know that children are highly attuned to inconsistency. Teenagers, in particular, stand at the ready to shout "hypocrite" at adults who fail to practice what they preach.

David Abram encountered precisely this challenge one evening. Things at David's legal practice usually went fairly smoothly, but between challenging clients and a difficult partners' meeting that day, David was almost maxed out. By the time he navigated the traffic home, he was at his limit.

Ben, Jonny, and Lisa had been waiting for David to have dinner, and they were eager to eat when he arrived. So eager, in fact, that in the first five minutes of dinner, nine-year-old Lisa whined repeatedly for food and then spilled her milk on her brother Jonny's lap. Jonny jumped up from his chair and screamed some choice words at his sister, who immediately burst into tears. In fact, Ben was the only child at the table who did not seem to be causing a commotion.

David finally lost it. He yelled at Lisa for whining, berated Jonny for insulting his sister, and reprimanded all the kids for ruining his dinner after he had such a difficult day at the office.

By a bit later that evening, David had recovered his balance. He noticed Ben and Jonny sitting on the couch looking sullen, and he sat down next to them:

"Guys, I know I got frustrated and yelled too much tonight. I always tell you to treat each other nicely, and what I did tonight probably seemed hypocritical. The truth is, I do owe all of you an apology. I believe we all need to treat each other nicely, and I try my best to do that as well. Tonight you saw me mess up. Not because I don't really believe in this, but because all of us come up short sometimes. When we do, we need to do our best to make it right, and to make sure we do better in the future."

In these few words, David demonstrates to his sons that falling short on occasion makes us human, not hypocritical.

David transforms a failure into an opportunity to model humility, sensitivity, and persistence. In doing so, he points us to a reassuring truth: You do not need to be perfect to be a perfect role model.

If we are conscious of our deep values, and if we live our commitments and relationships in a way that coincides with our values, it is a good bet that our children will do the same.

Chapter Seven

Practice, Practice, Practice

L et the teaching begin!

We have explored learning about our children, building relationships, and modeling behaviors and values. But we know that most concerned parents have been waiting for the part where they get to *teach* their children directly.

We will continue to see that direct teaching is only a small part of educating our children. Yet such teaching does indeed play a vital role, and it is crucial that we do it right.

What are the key principles of teaching our children?

The educational philosopher John Dewey was fond of using a simple image to get at the core of the question: Imagine that you are a camp counselor and your task is to teach a group of campers to swim. To be clear, the goal is not simply that they learn the doggie paddle, but rather that they become truly proficient swimmers, masters of a variety of strokes and techniques.

As a dedicated counselor, you research the scientific concepts that hold the key to swimming, including buoyancy, propulsion, drag, and Newton's three laws of motion. You then prepare a series of thorough lessons on each of these concepts and their application to the various swimming strokes. The campers study hard for their comprehensive final exam and they pass with flying colors.

Yet if any of the same campers should venture down to the camp pool on their own, the results would be quite different.

Teaching children to swim by lecturing in a classroom is obviously absurd. We know that the only way to learn to swim is to practice in a pool. But when it comes to educating our children, many of us fall into exactly this pattern. We are drawn toward telling our children how to behave, complete with logic, explanations, and rationale. When we ask our children what they are supposed to do, they can supply the correct answer. However, when it comes to real-life scenarios, the results are again quite different.

MORAL DILEMMAS

Consider the experience of Lawrence Kohlberg, the Harvard psychologist whose stages of moral development we discussed in Chapter 3.

Kohlberg and his colleagues assessed children's moral development by asking them to respond to a series of moral dilemmas, such as the Heinz Dilemma we read about earlier. In the course of this research, one of Kohlberg's students, Moshe Blatt, found something striking. The dilemmas designed to identify a child's stage of moral development did more than just illuminate the child's reasoning, they actually impacted it. In fact, Blatt's research demonstrated that engaging in ongoing discussion of moral dilemmas over time had a measurable positive effect on children's moral development.[1]

Educators greeted this finding with a great deal of excitement. Teachers who wanted to stimulate their students' moral growth now had a research-proven way to do so. Curricula were written, teacher manuals were created, and the Blatt-Kohlberg method was implemented in numerous schools.[2] By and large, teachers saw their students use increasingly complex moral reasoning in classroom discussions.

However, within a couple of years, teachers began to notice that their students' growth was limited to the theoretical realm. Students who had gained the ability to navigate complex moral scenarios in a classroom discussion were no less likely to cheat on their math test or get into a fight at recess. In other words, the students were learning how to *talk* about moral dilemmas, but they were not learning to act morally.

Teachers turned to Kohlberg for help. At first, attempts at improvement focused on the content of the dilemmas. Kohlberg suggested that if students discussed scenarios more closely related to their own daily experiences, they would be more likely to apply theory to practice. Despite the adjusted dilemmas, however,

---

1. In his initial research, Blatt found that twelve weeks of dilemma discussion led students to grow by a full stage beyond that of the control group. Later replications of the experiment found that students grew by approximately one-third of a stage in the same period, as compared to the control group. See the full description of his study in Moshe Blatt and Lawrence Kohlberg, "The Effects of Classroom Moral Discussion upon Children's Level of Moral Judgment," *Journal of Moral Education* 4, no. 2 (1975): 129–61.

2. For an overall analysis of the progression of Kohlbergian methods, including both dilemma discussion and "Just Community" models, see F. Clark Power, Ann Higgins, and Lawrence Kohlberg, *Lawrence Kohlberg's Approach to Moral Education* (New York: Columbia University Press, 1989) and Joseph Reimer, Diane Paolitto, and Richard H. Hersh, *Promoting Moral Growth: From Piaget to Kohlberg*, 2nd ed. (New York: Longman, 1983).

students could not seem to connect the morning's theoretical discussion about cheating to their actual decision to cheat on the same afternoon's math test.

"JUST COMMUNITY" SCHOOLS

As teachers continued to express concerns, Kohlberg finally learned the lesson of the swimming class. He realized that to develop moral behavior, students must be given the opportunity to practice moral behavior. And so the "Just Community" school was born.[3]

Rather than limit discussion to the classroom, the entire school would now be a model for moral learning. At the center of the school was a justice committee whose majority was made up of student members. At a weekly schoolwide town hall meeting, the committee would hear arguments from students and faculty on any moral issues at play in school life. These might range from instances of cheating, to drug use, to general discipline policies, and the committee had full decision-making power up to the point of adjudicating student-expulsion hearings.

Teachers and students alike reported a greater engagement in the moral life of these schools. Students did not just discuss theoretical moral dilemmas, they debated real-life situations and, most importantly, they acted on their conclusions.[4] In creating the Just Community schools, Kohlberg provided the opportunity for moral practice. In other words, he had figured out how to move his young swimmers from the classroom to the pool.

---

3. See preceding note.
4. For a compelling portrayal of one Jewish school's journey through the phases of moral education, see Earl Schwartz, "Three Stages of a School's Moral Development," *Religious Education* 96, no. 1 (2001): 106–18.

Kohlberg created this paradigm shift in a school setting. How can we create a similar opportunity for real-life practice in our own homes?

The shift begins with a change in perspective. Bringing his swimming image to a head, John Dewey tells teachers, "Cease conceiving of education as mere preparation for later life, and make it the full meaning of the present life."[5] Parents, too, must understand that every moment of our children's family-life experience represents a chance to practice the values, skills, and habits that we hope will guide their lives.

MEALS AND MORALS

While some of these moments are scattered through our day, most of us already have our own "town hall meeting" on a routine basis in the form of our family dinner. The power of the family dinner is well documented. Studies have repeatedly shown that children who regularly eat dinner with their families tend to earn better grades in school and on standardized tests. Eating meals together has a greater impact on academic performance than does doing homework, and eating with your children will increase their vocabulary more than reading to them![6]

Though less easily quantifiable, research has also shown that children who eat dinner with their parents exhibit lower levels of stress, engage in fewer risk-taking behaviors, and tend to have more positive peer relationships and family relationships.

What is so powerful about Monday night's spaghetti and meatballs?

---

5. John Dewey, *Early Works*, vol. 4 (Carbondale: Southern Illinois University Press, 1967), 50.
6. For a summary of a portion of these studies, see http://ectutoring.com/resources/ articles/family-dinners-improve-students-grades (accessed July 22, 2015).

Researchers point to the family dinner as an opportunity for warm conversation framed around a relaxing conclusion to the day. The supportive connected atmosphere provides children with consistent emotional support and reinforcement. Emotionally healthy children who know that their parents are invested in their success are more likely to engage in positive behaviors and pursue academic success.

This is no doubt true. But it is not the whole story.

Take the finding about vocabulary. Keep in mind that the study not only found increases in children's vocabulary. It found that eating meals together generated *greater* increases than did reading to your children. But why? Factors such as emotional support and positive attitude are unlikely to lead to direct vocabulary improvement. And even if they did, a quiet evening reading on the couch should provide just as much emotional support as a nice family dinner.

ACTIVE PARTICIPATION

To see why a family dinner might be more impactful than a reading session, watch what happens in each type of interaction.

When Rachel was younger, one of Dan Stein's favorite activities was reading to his daughter. As soon as Dan got home in the evening, Rachel would run to get her favorite book. They would settle in on the couch, and Rachel would listen contently as Dan read through the next chapter. These moments provided an opportunity for father-daughter bonding, and helped engender a love of reading.

David and Sara Abram also loved reading to their children, but for them the family dinner was the most important part of each evening. Regardless of the menu, the routine was the same. Each of the Abram children took a turn sharing what had happened to them that day. They would engage each other in conversation, sharing experiences and asking questions. David and Sara would often step in to explain when one of the younger children did not understand something an older sibling had described.

If you think back to our swimming story, the key difference between these scenarios becomes obvious. During the reading session only Dan is active. Rachel sits contently and listens. She develops a bond with her father and appreciates the time they have together. Yet any learning she does is entirely passive. Rachel does not question, engage, or in any other way *practice* new language skills during these sessions. Hearing her father read does enhance Rachel's vocabulary, but the impact is limited by her lack of active engagement.

What is true about vocabulary holds true for every area of our children's development. As they interact with siblings and parents at the dinner table, children have a crucial opportunity to practice language, social, and emotional skills.

WHAT KIND OF DINNER?

Of course not every family dinner provides the same level of benefit. For example, obesity researchers often focused their studies on comparing families that ate dinner together with those that did not. These studies indicated that family dinners lead to healthier eating habits for children. But this was not enough for pediatrician and researcher Jerica Berge. She wanted to understand *why* eating meals together seemed to prevent youth obesity.

To answer this question, Berge and her team studied a group of families that ate dinner together at least three times a week.[7] Contrary to the conventional wisdom, half of these families included children who were overweight or obese. The researchers'

---

7. Jerica Berge et al. "Childhood Obesity and Interpersonal Dynamics During Family Meals," *Pediatrics*, http://pediatrics.aappublications.org/content/early/2014/10/08/peds.2014-1936 (accessed May 10, 2015).

task was to figure out why eating together worked for some families but not others.

Berge's team recorded each family's dinners over the course of an eight-day period. They then painstakingly coded every interaction at each meal. What they found was striking. Almost without exception, the meals of families with overweight or obese children were accompanied by negative interactions, minimal communication, and controlling parental behavior. Families whose children were within a healthy weight range had meals characterized by a warm supportive atmosphere that included more communication. These families spent a longer time around the table together as well. The research team concluded that it was specifically the warm, supportive atmosphere during these family dinners that influenced children's overall emotional health, and by extension their eating habits.

What Berge saw in the positive family dinners could best be characterized as positive, structured interactions. The negative family dinners were dominated by parental control, often including threats (e.g., if you do not eat well you won't be healthy). The positive dinners looked more like carefully coached communication. Children spoke frequently to siblings and parents, parents offered consistently positive reinforcement and gentle correction when necessary. Based on what we have learned, it is safe to suggest that the positive dinner table was not only a supportive environment but also a practice field for learning healthy, interpersonal relations, with the children taking center stage and the parents seamlessly guiding their development.

COMING HOME

The dinner table is the most obvious but by no means the only place where our children practice. Much of their practice takes the form of daily patterns that fall below our conscious radar.

Adam Stein comes home from school tired and often in a bad mood. While Debbie knows that she should be happy to see her son at the end of the day, lately she has come to dread the moment that Adam walks in, slams the front door, and throws his backpack on the floor. Within minutes Adam has found a reason to growl at his sister. Debbie steps in to put Adam in his place and the calm afternoon quickly turns into a fight. Debbie's friends reassure her that it is just a stage. Teenagers are all difficult, and Adam will grow out of this behavior eventually.

Debbie's friends are correct. The teenage years are a challenging stage for everyone, and Adam may grow out of this particular behavior. Yet the fundamental pattern he is learning will likely repeat itself later in life. It is all too easy to imagine adult Adam coming home at the end of a long day at the office. He has outgrown slamming the door and throwing his briefcase on the floor. But his family dreads his entrance just the same. They know that if there is a toy out of place, if the table is not set for dinner, or if anything else does not meet his expectations, Adam will snap at them. They have come to expect at least one argument before dinner most nights of the week.

BENEATH THE RADAR

Debbie is not at fault for adult Adam's behavior. But if she sees each afternoon as an opportunity for practice, she may be able to help her son develop healthier patterns when he is still a teen. Let's look at what Debbie does *not* see each day as Adam arrives home.

Adam boards the bus at school and sits with his friends. It is a short ride and they enjoy joking around together as they blow off steam at the end of the day. The bus stops at Adam's street and he gets off still smiling and laughing. As he walks the 50 feet from the bus to his front door, the corners of Adam's smile start to turn downwards. He opens the front door and surveys the situation.

Mom is in the family room working on the computer, his sister Rachel is in the kitchen having a snack and doing her homework. No one seems to have noticed his arrival. Even as he slams the door they barely seem to move. Adam stomps into the kitchen and tells Rachel she's doing her homework wrong. Rachel whines for her mom, and Debbie is suddenly up from the computer and yelling at Adam. He finally has their attention

Let's be clear. It is not Debbie's fault that Adam has chosen to seek attention this way. She does not need to be at the front door waiting for Adam, cookies and milk in hand. At the same time, the family home is the arena where Adam is learning behavioral patterns. As a parent, Debbie has the crucial ability to adjust the rules of the game to shape Adam's practice.

MANAGING TRANSITIONS

We know that big changes are difficult. We understand that our children may need support as they move to a new city or as they shift schedules from summer vacation back to school. Minor transitions can be challenging as well. Even coming home at the end of the day can produce a phenomenon that psychologists refer to as burning up on re-entry. This kind of transition is often all the more challenging because we take it for granted. Coming home to relax after a day at work or school should be the easy part!

It is precisely this phenomenon that is at play in Adam's daily routine. He does well at school, and eventually he does well at home too, yet crossing the threshold from one to the other is stressful. Adam needs emotional support during this transition. As a fifteen-year-old, Adam may not know how to ask for help. In his own teenage way, he has figured out a way to get the emotional attention that he craves. Unfortunately, left to his own devices he has found that the easiest way to satisfy his anxiety is by eliciting negative responses.

Each day Adam practices getting this kind of reaction from his mother and sister. He becomes more and more adept at creating the whirlwind of negative energy that satisfies his emotional needs.

Scolding, reprimanding, or punishing Adam is unlikely to change this pattern. But what if Debbie changes the rules of the game?

Adam opens the front door and surveys the situation. Mom is in the family room working on the computer, and Rachel is in the kitchen having a snack and doing her homework. The minute she hears Adam come in, Debbie calls out to him, "How was your day? Come in here for a minute, I want to check in with you." Adam pauses. He thinks about slamming the door but instead walks over to the family room to talk to his mother.

With this small adjustment to the afternoon routine, Debbie influences Adam's pattern. She preempts his negative behavior by allowing him to practice getting the attention he needs as a result of entering the house calmly.

LEAST REINFORCING SYNDROME

Of course Debbie may not always be able to preempt negative behavior:

Adam opens the front door and surveys the situation...No one seems to have noticed his arrival...Adam tells Rachel she's doing her homework wrong...Rachel whines and mom is suddenly up from the computer.

But Debbie understands what Adam is doing. She ushers Rachel quietly into the other room. Neither Debbie nor Rachel reacts to Adam in this moment. Adam sulks a bit more and slams his school books on the table, which is not very satisfying. Finally he sits down to do his homework. Once Adam is sitting quietly, Debbie walks over, asks him about his day, and offers him a snack.

To the untrained eye, it may seem that Debbie has simply avoided an issue or is neglecting her parental duties by not reprimanding Adam. In truth she has fundamentally changed the rules of the game by utilizing a technique called "least reinforcing syndrome."[8]

Adam struggles with coming home each afternoon. Subconsciously, he is looking for emotional support to ease the challenge of this transition. The problem is that when we need such support, we tend not to differentiate between positive and negative emotional energy. For children, teens, or adults under emotional stress, *any* strong reaction is gratifying. The more intense the reaction, the more gratifying it feels. Unfortunately, the easiest way to generate powerful reactions in others is to upset them. Our natural tendency will be to poke and prod those around us until we get the emotional response we need.

When she sees Adam poking his sister, Debbie's task is to ensure that his behavior does *not* elicit a reinforcing response of any sort. It is only when Adam has resumed appropriate behavior that Debbie gives him the emotional response he craves. If she can hold to this approach and muster the self-control to ignore Adam's prodding, Debbie will successfully change the rules of the game. Adam's playing field will be one that supplies emotional satisfaction only in response to positive behaviors. By practicing on this field, he will learn to respond to stress by seeking positive attention rather than by using negative provocations.[9]

---

8. This and other interesting behavior-modification approaches were brought to the mainstream in Amy Sutherland's insightful and amusing *New York Times* article, "What Shamu Taught Me About a Happy Marriage," http://www.nytimes.com/2006/06/25/fashion/25love.html?pagewanted=all&_r=0 (accessed July 22, 2015).

9. This approach is closely related to how we approach the topic of discipline, which we will address directly in Chapter 8.

In the same way, every aspect of the family dynamic provides a similar opportunity for our children to practice interpersonal skills. The way we shape the playing field will determine what they learn.

MITZVA PRACTICE

The concept of practice applies beyond the interpersonal realm. As devoted Jewish parents, we want our children to develop both a sense of faith and a commitment to religious practice.

The mitzva of lulav for the festival of Sukkot illustrates the case of mitzva practice beautifully. A kosher lulav-and-etrog set can cost anywhere from $50 to $250 depending on market prices and the quality of the set. Purchasing one for yourself may be reasonable. Multiply the cost by a number of children and it can strain the budget of most families.

Concerned parents often approach their rabbi with a question: Do we really need to buy a kosher lulav for our ten-year-old? He has not even reached bar mitzva yet, and an "almost kosher" set would be significantly cheaper without looking any different to the child.

The halakhic sources present a striking response. As the rabbi will inevitably explain, if a family cannot afford to purchase more than one lulav, there are most certainly ways for parents to "share" a single set with their children, and no family is obligated to purchase the highest-priced set in the store. Purchasing an "almost kosher" set, however, is not an acceptable solution. In the words of one medieval rabbinic commentator, "when we train a child in mitzvot, we must have him fulfill the mitzva in the proper manner as would an adult."[10]

---

10. Commentary of Ritva on Sukka 2a, s.v. *Amar Rav Yehuda*. See, as well, *Shulḥan Arukh, Oraḥ Ḥayim* 657, and commentary of *Biur Halakha* there.

Parents are often surprised (and disappointed) by the rabbi's response. If the child is still a minor, why do we need to stretch our budget to buy him a fully kosher lulav?

This question is all the more fraught when we realize that there are indeed areas of Jewish law where we are more lenient with a minor. In the same discussions, for example, some authorities note that while adults cannot fulfill their obligation on the first day of Sukkot with a borrowed lulav, a child can in fact do so. In terms of its physical properties, however, even these authorities agree that the lulav must be fully kosher.[11]

AUTHENTICITY

The message here seems quite clear. If we take our children's religious experience seriously, we must enable them to engage in authentic practice. Playing with toys or imitation mitzva objects will not lead to serious engagement. While some accommodation to the surrounding circumstances can be made, such as permitting a borrowed lulav, children fundamentally must be allowed to work with the real tools of religious practice.[12]

The Reggio Emilia approach to early childhood education, which represents best practices in supporting children's holistic development and critical thinking, takes a similar tack.[13] This approach, developed in and around the town of Reggio Emilia in Italy following World War II, sees early childhood as a crucial time for personality development. To support their development, the Reggio Emilia approach insists, young children should be treated

---

11. *Yalkut Yosef* to *Kitzur Shulḥan Arukh, Oraḥ Ḥayim* 658.
12. See Sukka 42a, which suggests that parents must provide their children not only with a lulav but with other mitzva objects, such as tefillin and tzitzit, as well, as soon as the child is physically able to handle these objects.
13. Carla Rinaldi, whose response to the "moon question" we referenced in Chapter 1, is a leading figure in the Reggio Emilia inspired approach.

with the same respect as adults and given meaningful responsibility as they learn by exploring the environment around them.[14]

In Reggio Emilia type schools, whether in Italy or elsewhere, you will not see toddlers using disposable utensils or sippy cups. Nor will you see teachers pouring the milk for two-year-olds at snack time. The classrooms are filled with real furniture and adult utensils, down to the glass pitchers used for milk. At the same time, however, these authentic items are shaped in a way that is appropriate for young children. Glass pitchers are used, but only the 16-ounce size, so that children can pour for themselves. Wooden tables and chairs, like those in an adult dining room, are used instead of colorful plastic play-furniture. But they too are sized appropriately for smaller arms and legs.

The Reggio Emilia classroom is a living metaphor for what we seek in mitzva practice – authentic objects and real mitzva experiences that are sized appropriately for our children. We purchase a kosher lulav for our children, but we do not force them to attend the full length of an extended holiday synagogue-service. We help them create their own cups for Friday night Kiddush, patterned after the adult version but sized appropriately for small hands. We help our teenagers create a teen minyan for Shabbat morning prayers, including all the elements of the adult service but with an appropriate pace and tone for a teenage attention span.

FAITH EXPERIENCES

In Chapter 3 we met James Fowler, the Harvard psychologist who analyzed and outlined the stages of faith development. We often think of faith as a specific or separate area of our religious lives. The crux of Fowler's work challenges this understanding.

---

14. For more background on the Reggio Emilia approach and its current applications, see http://reggioalliance.org/, accessed December 11, 2015.

Fowler teaches us that "faith is a person or group's way of moving into the force field of life. It is our way of finding coherence in and giving meaning to the multiple forces and relations that make up our lives. Faith is a person's way of seeing him- or herself in relation to others against a background of shared meaning and purpose."[15]

If faith is how we understand the world around us and the best teaching occurs through practice, then teaching faith means helping our children practice understanding the world. Authentic and age-appropriate mitzva observance provides a natural opportunity for this kind of practice.

As the Abram family begins preparing for Jonny's bar mitzva, they realize that he will need a set of tefillin. It would be easiest to purchase a finished set at the local Jewish bookstore or even to order one from Israel. But David has something else in mind. He knows that this is an opportunity to engage Jonny on a deeper level. So David seeks out the local *sofer* (scribe) and makes an unusual request. Rather than presenting Jonny with a completed set, David arranges for himself and his son to sit with the *sofer* as he writes out the Torah portions on parchment and assembles the tefillin.

The experience provides Jonny with a deeper understanding of the mitzva and a personal connection to his tefillin. Perhaps more important, as they sit with the *sofer* for the afternoon, father and son come to discuss why we wear tefillin and what this mitzva has meant to David over the years. Jonny naturally begins to integrate the meaning of tefillin into his own view of the world.

While a child receives new tefillin only once in his lifetime, other mitzvot offer similar opportunities on a daily basis. Take, for

---

15. James Fowler, *Stages of Faith* (San Francisco: Harper San Francisco, 1981), 4.

example, the mitzva of learning Torah. If we approach it correctly, the act of learning together with our children constitutes both the practice of a specific mitzva and an organic time to discuss the meaning of Torah and mitzvot. Our children will naturally connect these discussions to their developing faith as they participate actively in the learning experience.

Beyond specific mitzvot and Torah learning, the ups and downs of everyday life offer the chance to practice faith with our children. Think back to David and Sara's discussion with Ben after Holocaust Remembrance Day. Ben is deeply troubled by what he has learned. While they are not happy to see their son struggle, David and Sara know that this is an opportunity to engage with him. As they support and guide him, they give him the chance to practice his faith and deepen his understanding of the world.

The same holds true for when our child comes home thrilled that her team won the soccer championship, inspired by her school's Shabbaton retreat program, or crushed at having just failed an important test. As parents, we can respond to each of these moments as a personal accomplishment/struggle. Or, we can realize that these charged experiences open a window into our children's inner-emotional state and create a unique opportunity to engage with our children in the practice of faith development.[16]

---

16. It was perhaps this phenomenon, related to both the highs and lows of life, that the Talmud had in mind when it instructed us, "A person must bless God for the bad just as he blessed God for the good" (Berakhot 33b).

Chapter Eight

Discipline and Development

We have learned about playing with our children, connecting, role modeling, and practicing. All of that is relatively easy when the kids are behaving well. Of course David and Sara Abram have wonderful relationships with their children. Their kids always seem to be acting nicely.

But what are we supposed to do when our kids do not behave? How should we react when they rebel, act out, or are just plain difficult?

The truth is, some children will be more demanding than others, and some days will be difficult while others are a breeze. At some point, all children will challenge us. How we respond to these challenges determines what happens next.

Even the Abram kids are no exception to this rule. Remember the struggles of twelve-year-old Ben Abram. His middle school disorganization led to daily reprimands, reminders, nagging, and fighting. Sara was frustrated and did not know how to fix her son's behavior.

Earlier we focused on the difference between Sara's first attempts to intervene directly and her later, more successful, indirect interventions. Now let's rewind to Ben's middle school years and zoom in on another aspect of this unfolding scenario.

SHIFTING PERSPECTIVE

Each afternoon, as the clock nears 5:00 p.m. and Ben is about to return home, Sara feels her blood pressure start to rise. She has already had a full day at work and has started to resent the daily routine of fighting with her son. Why can't he just get himself together? It's not just that he can't remember his assignments, now Ben even gets angry when Sara tries to remind him. Naturally, Sara finds this infuriating. She becomes more and more upset with Ben.

When our children misbehave, they make our lives more difficult. They may ruin an outing, add unnecessary frustration to our day, or say things that are hurtful and upsetting. Yet the anger we so naturally feel at those moments can sabotage our attempts to parent effectively.

This is the irony of discipline. We are most likely to be upset with our children at these challenging moments. Yet the first step in appropriate discipline is to put our natural anger aside. Sara Abram's frustration with Ben led her to approach the problem straight on by reminding, nagging, and berating him. Neither of them was happy, and Ben's habits still showed no sign of changing.

Often one parent becomes more embroiled in the conflict than the other. In this case, because Sara was more organized and punctilious than her husband, David, she was knee-deep in frustration with her son's issues. For his part, David was not happy that Ben forgot his homework, but such shortcomings simply did not strike the same emotional chord for him.

They had lived in this negative cycle for several months. One evening David tried to talk it through with Sara.

> *David:* I know Ben's been really frustrating lately.
> *Sara:* I don't know what's gotten into him. He used to be such an easy kid to deal with. Now everything's a fight.
> *David:* Do you think we can do something for him?
> *Sara:* Honestly, I don't know anymore. The first step is for him to get a hold of himself. He simply cannot speak to me the way he does and expect me to help him. He's become arrogant and just rude. This needs to start with him apologizing for how he's been acting lately.

Sara is explaining her struggles with Ben in the same way as she would view a confrontation with another adult. In a conflict between two adults, the one who is primarily at fault bears responsibility for initiating the resolution. The problem is that this is not a conflict between two adults. The pendulum of parental duty swings only one way.

This does not mean that children don't need to learn responsibility in their own lives. But as far as discipline is concerned, parents will only be successful if we understand that the solution begins with us.

CHOICE THEORY

The turning point for Sara comes when she broadens her own thinking. Stepping back from her feelings of frustration, Sara finally asks herself, "What else can I do to help my son?" To a neutral observer, this is a simple step in the problem-solving process. To an exasperated parent like Sara, it is a difficult yet crucial transition.

We may be able to ease the difficulty if we paint a different picture of what discipline problems mean. Consider the perspective put forth by Dr. William Glasser in what he calls choice theory.[1] According to Glasser's theory, all human behavior can be explained by a single rationale: "We always choose to do what is most satisfying to us at the time."[2]

At first read, this notion seems completely self-serving. Imagine justifying your own behavior this way: "Sorry, Officer, stealing that car was just the most satisfying thing to do at the moment." "I understand. If it was the most satisfying, I guess I'll have to let it slide." But when Glasser applies the theory to children, it starts to make more sense.

Our children, Glasser says, do not misbehave because of any pernicious motive. Most of us would agree with this assertion. We tend to believe that our children are kind and good-natured. Why, then, does our kind-hearted son kick his younger brother? Why does our sweet thirteen-year-old respond to her mother with biting sarcasm?

Every individual has an array of needs. We are naturally driven to seek satisfaction for those needs. As adults we may look to relationships, family, or professional involvements for gratification. Children who act out are simply trying, however misguidedly, to achieve the same end.

When our baby cries, we instinctively know that he is not misbehaving. The baby just needs something. The same is true, Glasser suggests, when our son misbehaves or our daughter snaps at us. Our job as parents is to figure out just what that need may be, and to help our children fulfill their needs in a productive and healthy manner. If we can bring this perspective to bear, we will

---

1. Choice theory was originally called "control theory," a name that did not earn it many friends. Even with the updated name, Glasser's theory has met with significant criticism in the world of psychological research. Nonetheless, his perspective is helpful in our efforts to balance some of our natural tendencies.
2. William Glasser, *Choice Theory in the Classroom* (New York: HarperCollins, 1986), 21.

find that it fundamentally reshapes how we think about these challenging moments with our children.

DEFINING NEEDS

Understanding what we mean by "need" is crucial to applying Glasser's approach. A baby's needs tend to be fairly easy to ascertain. Once we have cycled through the hungry, wet, and tired options, we have most likely identified the issue. As children grow, their needs become more varied and complex. Glasser suggests that human needs fall into five basic categories: the needs "(1) to survive and reproduce, (2) to belong and love, (3) to gain power, (4) to be free, and (5) to have fun."[3]

We would all agree that survival and reproduction should be classified as basic needs. The other categories in Glasser's list may be more surprising. Even if we agree that humans have a need for love and belonging, do we really have a need for fun? Would that not be better categorized as a want, a desire, or a luxury?

Glasser's response is an emphatic no. His definition of "need" is not limited to that which is required for basic functioning. "Needs" encompass every area that deeply influences our behavior. Even if we disagree with the terminology, we cannot argue with the phenomenon. Children's behavior is often motivated not only by basic physical needs but also by their desire to belong, to feel a sense of power and control, and, of course, to have fun.

And so, when we see our child kicking a younger sibling or being rude, we must ask ourselves what "need" the child is trying to satisfy. A need for attention? A need to feel powerful? A need for emotional stimulation? We may feel that our children should not have these needs. But telling a child not to need attention or power is as useless as telling a baby not to need a nap. Instead of

---

3. Glasser, *Choice Theory in the Classroom*, 25.

demanding that our kids overcome their natural tendencies, as we saw Sara do in her conversation with David, the only way to change our children's behavior is to first uncover the need which is the underlying cause of their actions.

Please do not misunderstand. The fact that children's misbehavior is based on unmet needs does not mean that the parents' task is simply to meet all of their needs. Rather, recognizing the sources of challenging behavior allows us to develop an appropriate strategy for helping our children learn to meet their own needs more effectively. Let's illustrate with some concrete examples.

INTERVENTION STRATEGIES

The most direct strategy is to provide an immediate opportunity for the child to fulfill his need in a productive manner. If our son is kicking his younger sibling out of boredom, redirecting him to help set the table for dinner, read his new book, or work on a school project gives him a way to satisfy his need without hurting anyone in the process.

With each redirection of this kind, we help our child to practice finding healthy ways to satisfy the need for stimulation. And we do not need to wait for the problem before we come up with a solution. Knowing that late afternoon is a challenging time that tends to be filled with whining or fighting among siblings, we may choose to lay out our children's favorite games in advance to redirect their energies before the complaints begin. Establishing this kind of routine or structure enables our children to develop healthy patterns in meeting their own needs.[4]

---

4. In many ways this is simply the flip-side of the Least Reinforcing Syndrome we saw in the previous chapter. The goal of the LRS approach is to prevent individuals from meeting their needs for attention or power in an unhealthy manner.

Sara faces a similar challenge in dealing with Ben's disorganization. As she eventually moves from confrontation to support, Sara asks herself how she can help her son. The answer, of course, is to first identify Ben's needs. To be clear, we do not mean Ben's need to get good grades or his need to hand his homework in on time. These may be requirements, goals, or responsibilities, or they may be his parents' needs, but they are not Ben's needs. We mean the underlying emotional needs: Ben's desire to feel a sense of mastery, competence, and power within his personal sphere.

As soon as we reframe the challenge in this way, we see why Sara's initial reaction was self-defeating. Sara tried to intervene directly. She bought Ben an agenda and told him to use it, reminded him to empty out his backpack, and even sat down to do his homework with him. Each of these well-meaning interventions disempowered Ben, making it less and less likely that he would achieve his emotional needs. Very few twelve-year-olds feel proud about handing in homework their mother did for them. And so it is no surprise that Ben pushed back rudely against Sara's reminders in an effort to preserve power in his personal sphere.

Ultimately Sara steps back from these direct interventions. Instead she focuses on setting the stage for Ben to be successful by adjusting his transportation and class schedule. This combination of personal space and a supporting structure is exactly what Ben needs. Sara has positioned him to meet his needs for mastery, competence, and power by succeeding through his own initiative.

PUNISHMENTS

Most parents are with us up to this point. Yet they still need to ask: What about the consequences? It seems unfair for my child to get away with misbehaving. If there are no consequences for negative behavior, how will my child learn?

Before we respond to this question, we need to clarify what we mean by "consequences." In past generations, conventional wisdom dictated that misbehavior deserved punishment. As the old adage went, "spare the rod and spoil the child." Thankfully, corporal punishment is no longer considered an appropriate form of discipline. More than that, even the word "punishment" evokes negative associations for most of us. Popular culture has come to believe that punishments need to be replaced by consequences.[5]

Advocates of this approach like to note that, unlike punishments, consequences are simply the natural ramifications of our children's behavior. This sounds enticing. But take a closer look at how it plays out in practice.[6]

Twelve-year-old Jonny Abram loves to hang out with his friends during long summer afternoons and weekends. He is barely in the door from day camp when he jumps back on his bike to go meet up with his friends. This is new for Jonny and the Abrams are adjusting to his recently developed sense of freedom and independence. They give him permission to go out as long as he remembers to use his cell phone to call them when he arrives at his destination.

The problem is that Jonny usually forgets to call. By the time Sara has grown worried enough to call him, Jonny is involved in some game and has left his phone off to the side. When he returns home, Sara is concerned, frustrated, and upset. She feels like punishing Jonny by sending him to bed early.

---

5. Approaches such as assertive discipline and cooperative discipline have largely influenced this change in terminology.
6. Articles and websites advocating for and explaining the consequences approach abound. The vast majority of them take a very similar tack. Our scenario borrows from a typical example that can be found at http://www.empoweringparents.com/punishments-vs-consequences-which-are-you-using.php#ixzz3hsfLfwsk (accessed August 3, 2015).

CONSEQUENCES

Here the advocates of the consequences approach step in. The punishment Sara is considering, they explain, is not related to Jonny's behavior. How will an early bedtime teach him to do better next time?

We would agree that the punishment doesn't match the crime, and that it will not teach Jonny to do better. Experience and research have both shown that it is unlikely to lead to any real change. Jonny missed his check-in call because remembering any appointment is a challenge for his disorganized pre-teen mind. Punishing him for not calling is like reprimanding him for not being taller.

Instead of this punishment, the consequences teachers say, Sara should try to think of an appropriate response related to Jonny's behavior. In this scenario they might suggest that if Jonny cannot use his freedom responsibly, he should not be allowed to go out with his friends this week. Jonny should be given a second chance next week, but only if he feels he can remember to call home.

Is this consequence fundamentally different from the punishment Sara was contemplating? Instead of sending Jonny to his room, Sara would be grounding him. She may even tell Jonny that she wants him to learn that privilege comes with responsibility, that it is a natural consequence for him to lose the chance to hang out with his friends when he does not check in as expected.

It would be wonderful for Jonny to learn responsibility as a result of this consequence. But despite Sara's explanation, he will not walk away having learned the lesson. More likely, Jonny will come to understand that his parents take away his privileges when he does not comply with their rules. This is a vital distinction. Parents may convince themselves that a consequence is a natural outcome, but the child experiences it as an external reinforcement imposed upon him.

Any lesson Jonny learns from being grounded will likely come with some resentment. Even if it does not, at best it can be compared to the child who touches a hot stove. The burn may teach him not to touch the stove again, but there is no cognitive, spiritual, or moral development that comes with this learned behavior.

DISCIPLINE FOR GROWTH

Though its proponents are very well-meaning, the consequence approach is based on a fundamental error. Imposing penalties on our children, whether in the form of punishments or consequences, *can* change their behavior. It cannot, however, force them to truly learn.

And what is it that we want our children to learn?

To be good and moral people. To lead productive, balanced, and healthy lives. To be spiritually sensitive and religiously committed. If these are our answers, then using the consequence approach will satisfy our own emotional need for power at the expense of our children's healthy development.

Consider an alternative approach that can support real growth. Take the same cell phone scenario: The problem is that Jonny usually forgets to call. By the time Sara has grown worried enough to call him, Jonny is involved in some game and has left his phone off to the side. When he returns home, Sara is concerned, frustrated, and upset. She feels like punishing Jonny by sending him to bed early.

Instead of getting worked up about how inconsiderate Jonny has been, Sara recognizes that the primary goal here is to ensure that Jonny is safe. That is a pragmatic concern which can be addressed by Jonny checking in, by Sara texting him when he is still en route with phone in hand, or by pre-arranging check-ins with Jonny's friends' parents in case he forgets. Knowing that she has backup systems in place, Sara can focus more clearly on Jonny's growth.

Sara does not just want Jonny to remember to call home. What she really wants is for him to learn that his actions affect those he cares about. Being responsible and conscientious means following through on his commitments. And so, when Jonny returns home after an outing without a check-in, Sara sits down with him to (calmly) share that she was worried. She explains that Jonny deserves to go out with his friends but that she also deserves to know he is safe.

Together they brainstorm ideas that can help in the future. Jonny suggests that he can set an alarm on his phone. Within a few minutes he has found a GPS app that will send him a reminder to call home every time he enters his favorite ice cream store.

By engaging Jonny in problem-solving rather than imposing a consequence, Sara has strengthened their relationship and helped him understand how his actions affect others. She has also given him an authentic opportunity to practice responsible behavior and has demonstrated how to set up structures (such as the GPS reminder) which will enable him to succeed. Rather than arousing resentment, this collaborative approach naturally generates buy-in, as it satisfies the child's need for empowerment.

STEPPING BACK

Note that the first step in this alternative approach is for us, as parents, to take a step back from our own emotions before responding to our children. Perhaps, if we have had a good day at work, recently had a snack or a cup of coffee, and did not hit any traffic on our way home, we may be able to put our concerns aside before dealing with our children's issues. But the reality is that our emotions often do get the best of us. There will be times when we snap at our children, when we threaten punishment (consequence), or when we just lose our cool.

It is at these times that the consequence approach can be most dangerous. Anger is like a freight train. The more momentum it builds, the more difficult it is to stop. When our temper begins to rise, we are confronted with a choice. We can engage in the challenging task of slowing the train. Or we can find a convenient rationalization that justifies our anger.

If we choose the latter, we are free to allow our emotions to reach their satisfying crescendo without worrying about too much guilt. Any parent who has been goaded by a three-year-old or a thirteen-year-old knows just how tempting it is to let our anger get the better of us. When that moment comes, the consequence approach starts to look a lot more appealing. "How else will they learn?" we tell ourselves. And with that we allow our emotions to boil over onto the offending child.

We all lose control sometimes. But we must resist the urge to tell ourselves that our anger is warranted as part of our parenting.

ANGER

And if we do feel that anger must be part of our parenting, we would do well to take the guidance of Maimonides before proceeding. In his discussion of character virtues, Maimonides typically recommends that we pursue a balanced approach as we attempt to embody the golden mean. Yet when it comes to anger he minces no words:

> Anger is also an exceptionally bad quality. It is fitting and proper that one move away from it and adopt the opposite extreme. He should school himself not to become angry even when it is fitting to be angry.
>
> If he should wish to arouse fear in his children and household – or within the community, if he is a communal

leader – and wishes to be angry at them to motivate them to return to the proper path, he should present an angry front to them to punish them, but he should be inwardly calm. He should be like one who acts out the part of an angry man in his wrath, but is not himself angry.[7]

In other words, Maimonides tells us, it may be appropriate to seem angry, but it is never appropriate to actually be angry. We may add that if we intend to seem angry for the sake of education, we must first take extra care to ensure that our anger is indeed only an appearance.

Although he uses the term "anger," what Maimonides describes may be more appropriately termed outrage. Unlike anger, outrage is a vital part of moral education.[8] If we are strongly committed to moral values, we must be outraged when those values are violated.

What is the difference between anger and outrage?

David Abram gets a call at work just as he is about to head home. According to the principal, Jonny, who is usually a good student, was caught cheating on a seventh-grade math test. David hangs up the phone, embarrassed and frustrated with his son. Fortunately he has some time to cool down on the drive before he gets home to talk to Jonny.

David takes a deep breath and walks into Jonny's room. He still wants to give Jonny a piece of his mind. But instead of letting his emotions loose on his son, David takes a serious but balanced tone. He tells Jonny that this sort of behavior is completely

7. Maimonides, *Mishneh Torah, Hilkhot De'ot* 2:3. Translation from http://www.chabad.org/library/article_cdo/aid/910342/jewish/Deot-Chapter-Two.htm (accessed May 20, 2015).

8. The role of outrage in moral education and leadership is presented effectively by Thomas J. Sergiovanni, *Moral Leadership: Getting to the Heart of School Improvement* (New York: Jossey Bass, 1992).

unacceptable. And he emphasizes that dishonesty has no place in their family, because they, including Jonny, are simply better than that. After some tears from Jonny, they talk more about what happened and what Jonny can change for the future.

The distinction between anger and outrage is not just about how loudly the parent yells. Anger is personally directed and diminishes the child. Outrage focuses on ideals and encourages the child to live up to those ideals. When we get angry, we do damage to our relationship. And we have learned that our relationship with our children is actually the most important factor in stimulating and guiding their growth. When we express outrage, we tell our children that because of our relationship we will not let them slip from the principles we hold dear. We show them that through our relationship we will support them in achieving those ideals.

RULES

Let's be clear. Arguing against consequences does not mean that we should not tell our children what to do. Nor does it mean that there should be no rules or expected routines in the household. But as we reflect on how to deal with children who break the rules, we need to give some thought to how we ourselves approach the rules.

The Steins believe that having a clear set of rules is the key to raising a good family. Adam and Rachel have both had strict bedtimes since they were old enough to turn on the TV by themselves. When the kids were younger, this meant Dan and Debbie ushering the kids upstairs at 8:45 each night. As Adam became a teenager, he began to negotiate for additional time, particularly when he wanted to go out with friends. When he entered tenth grade his curfew was set at 11:00 p.m.

Adam and Rachel also have daily chores to do around the house. They are expected to make their beds and to keep their rooms neat. Adam is tasked with taking out the garbage, and Rachel's job is to clear the table.

Adam and Rachel don't particularly like any of these chores, but their parents have made it clear that neither of them will get their weekly allowance if they do not complete their tasks. The kids don't love many of the other rules either, but they don't bother arguing, because, as the saying goes in their house, "a rule's a rule." And with that many a discussion has ended.

This approach allows the Steins to manage their family life efficiently. The children have learned to follow the rules without too much complaining. But compare this to what the Abram children learn from a slightly different approach.

At the end of a typical dinner in the Abram family, the children get up and take their plates over to the sink. If Ben or Jonny sees one of their parents starting to do the dishes, they will usually offer to help. Lisa tends toward helping make the lunches for the next day, and she starts to gather everyone's snacks. It's not that these kids like doing chores. It's that they feel an internal pull to help their parents.

After dinner the family takes to the den and starts to relax. When the kids were younger, this meant David or Sara reading to them on the couch. Now that they are older, they can read on their own, do their homework, or play a board game together. At around 9:00 p.m. each night, the younger kids wrap up and go to bed. The older ones usually go up at 11:00. They know that if they have a good reason to be up later, like the championship game on TV, David and Sara will make an exception. When Ben goes out with his friends on Saturday nights, his parents don't give him a curfew. Instead, David and Sara just ask Ben when he plans to be home. More often than not, he gives himself an earlier deadline than they would.

Ben, Jonny, and Lisa are fairly bright children. But ask any of them about their family rules and you will get a blank stare. Rules are externally imposed, often with a reward (allowance) or consequence attached. The Abram children don't believe that they live within a set of rules. They believe that they live in a family. And they are naturally compelled to act in a way that is generally considerate of everyone else in their family.

RELATIONSHIPS AND VALUES

Behavior choices in the Abram home are not guided by a need to conform to external rules but rather by relationships and values.[9] David and Sara are conscious of maintaining this focus. Whenever one of the children needs to help around the house or change their behavior, David and Sara frame the need in terms of consideration for others in the family (helping with the dishes) or commitment to values (going to bed so that you have energy for learning in school).

If you think back to Kohlberg's theory of moral development or Fowler's faith development, it is clear that this sort of approach naturally pulls our children toward higher stages of internally driven moral functioning. While rules educate toward conformity, organic expectations support growth and development.

Because it is imbued with inherent meaning, the Abram version of rules also tends to be self-enforcing. Children are intrinsically motivated to live up to their family's values.[10] When they fall short of the ideals they have grown to believe in, a heart-to-heart

---

9. Alfie Kohn outlines the possibility of a similar approach beyond the confines of the family in his description of the ideal classroom community in *Beyond Discipline* (Alexandria, VA: ASCD Press, 1996). The philosopher Nel Noddings describes a full system of ethics and moral education based on commitment to an ever-widening circle of relationships in *Caring* (Berkeley: University of California Press, 1984).

10. Assuming, of course, that parents have built strong relationships with their children.

discussion with a parent will be more powerful than any external consequence.

This broad approach to ideals is quite consonant with Jewish tradition. We often think of Jewish law as filled with intricate details. This is especially true when it comes to ritual law. Yet at the same time, the Torah is careful to emphasize the need for broad ideals to guide our behavior. These are best highlighted by the medieval commentator Nahmanides, who in his commentary on the Torah notes that biblical verses such as "love your neighbor as yourself"[11] and "you shall do the right and the good"[12] are intended to frame our approach to Jewish interpersonal law, infuse the law with meaning, and give credence to the all-important spirit of the law. In the realm of ritual law, Nahmanides notes that the verse "you shall be holy"[13] serves a similar function. While ritual law does contain more details, it is nonetheless vital that the law be framed within a larger context that provides the spirit behind each individual commandment.[14]

GLASSER AND FRANKL

At the beginning of this chapter we focused on the work of William Glasser. His explanation of human behavior as an attempt to satisfy our needs helps us frame our response to discipline. Yet Glasser's work can also be dangerous. It can be misunderstood as justifying stealing food to fulfill our need to eat, lying to meet our need for power, or satisfying our need for entertainment by hurting others' feelings.

---

11. Leviticus 19:18.

12. Deuteronomy 6:18.

13. Leviticus 19:2.

14. For an expanded application of this approach, see Walter Wurzburger's *Ethics of Responsibility: Pluralistic Approaches to Covenantal Ethics* (Philadelphia: Jewish Publication Society, 1994).

Glasser's work is an on-target description of the psychological drives that exist within us. Understanding this reality enables us to respond appropriately to our children. But the psychological reality provides no ethical justification for meeting our own needs in a way that violates our morals. The fact that we feel an urge does not give us the right to feed that urge.[15]

The best counterpoint to Glasser's work can be found in the work of the psychiatrist Viktor Frankl.[16] As a Holocaust survivor, Frankl lived through the horrors of the concentration camps and lost his wife in Bergen-Belsen. During his years of suffering, he searched for a way to transcend the conditions so viciously imposed upon him.

Frankl was deeply influenced by fellow inmates who retained their humanity in the most inhuman circumstances. Their ability to rise above their situation shaped his understanding of human behavior as diametrically opposed to Glasser's conclusions. Frankl vividly describes what he witnessed:

> We who lived in concentration camps can remember the men who walked through the huts comforting others, giving away their last piece of bread. They may have been few in number, but they offer sufficient proof that everything can be taken from a man but one thing: the last of the human

---

15. This principle, known in philosophy as Hume's law, argues that the existence of a certain reality, be it a psychological urge or a natural fact, does not mean that that reality is morally or ethically justified. Thus, the fact that we feel an emotional urge to meet our needs does not give us the moral right to meet those needs in any way we choose.

16. Viktor Frankl, *Man's Search for Meaning* (Boston: Beacon Press, 1984). For a popular application of Frankl's approach, see Stephen Covey's discussion of proactivity in *The Seven Habits of Highly Effective People* (New York: Simon & Schuster, 1989), Habit 1, 68 ff.

freedoms – to choose one's attitude in any given set of circumstances, to choose one's own way.[17]

Thankfully, most of us will never be placed in such horrifying circumstances. Yet Frankl explains that regardless of our situation, each of us faces an array of stimuli in our daily lives. These stimuli relate to what Glasser would call our needs: hunger, frustration, boredom, anger.

In contrast to Glasser, however, Frankl does not believe that these stimuli compel us to act. No matter how potent the provocation, we retain the power to choose our response. Because we have this power, we have a moral obligation to not simply react to our physical or emotional needs. Instead, we must process these stimuli, rise above them if necessary, and then act in a way that fits our ethical principles.

How is Frankl's work helpful to us as parents?

Glasser's theory allows us to understand why our children act out. Their misbehavior enables us to meet their needs so that we can help them grow. But ultimately we want this growth to lead our children to make moral choices in the manner that Frankl describes. Balancing these two perspectives enables us to help our children today while keeping a clear eye on where we want them to be in the future.

---

17. Frankl, *Man's Search for Meaning*, 86.

Chapter Nine

Culture and Context

What we described as the Abram family's approach to "rules" in the last chapter is part of a much larger picture. Everything that happens in a home is framed by the family's values, ideals, and commitments. These come together with more mundane family routines, habits, and choices to create what we call the family culture.

We are used to thinking of culture in terms of large groups based on nationality, religion, or ethnicity. Large-scale culture, in fact, provides a helpful lens to understand family culture.

When we travel to an exotic destination, we are quickly struck by cultural differences as we encounter new languages, modes of dress, food choices, popular entertainment, and social norms. We encounter analogous differences, though on a more nuanced level, when we interact with different communities closer to our own locale. Here the distinctions may be in the form of pronunciation rather than language or subtle preferences in fashion, cuisine, or media genre.

If we continue along this path, we will begin to notice that the same markers of culture exist within each family. The Steins and the Abrams may live a few blocks apart, attend the same schools, and have similar groups of friends. Yet if you look closely, you will no doubt see that the culture of each family is unique. The Steins prefer their food spicy, the Abrams have grown up eating sweeter dishes. The Abrams dress more formally, the Steins are most often in casual attire. The Steins have decorated their home with vividly colored paintings, the Abrams' wall hangings are understated.

As the list goes on, we begin to understand that each family does indeed have its own culture. Much of this culture is a matter of personal preferences developed over years, with no moral or ethical value. Spicy food will not lead to better-behaved children, casual attire will not lead to warmer family relationships.

Yet when we become aware of the nuances of each family's culture, we will uncover much that directs its children's growth in a subtle but powerful way. The manner in which a family approaches rules is just one example of this phenomenon. If we are conscious of these aspects of family life, which usually fade into the background, we can harness their power in shaping our children's development.[1]

LOCATION, LOCATION, LOCATION

To begin, let us consider several evening routines.

We have already learned about the power of the family dinner. But what happens after dinner is important as well.

---

1. In Chapter 6 we referred to the historian David Hackett Fischer. In addition to serving as an example for the power of role modeling, his research illuminates the myriad aspects of culture which any community or family passes on to coming generations. His work also documents the significant shaping power that this culture exerts on ethical life.

Like most families, the Steins had a lot to do most evenings. Adam and Rachel were usually busy with homework or catching up with friends. Dan and Debbie were finishing up household chores, answering work e-mails, and preparing for the next day. As soon as they finished dinner, the members of the Stein family would each head to their own corner of the home. The kids went to their bedrooms, Dan closed the door to his office, and Debbie was left alone in the living room.

Over time, the routine of everyone finding their own space became ingrained in the family culture. Even on nights when there was less work to do, on Sundays or on vacations, the Steins were most comfortable in their individual domains. This is not to say that they never spent time together. There were often family meals and activities that included the whole family. But when it came to down-time, they tended toward this individualistic culture.

The Abram family also had a lot to do each evening. Ben was busy with his youth group preparations, while Lisa and Jonny were typically doing homework and reading. David and Sara both had a lot of office paperwork to catch up on before the next day. As soon as they finished dinner in the kitchen, the family moved over to the dining room table, where they each started their work. As they wrapped up, they gradually moved over to the family room and settled down in their favorite spots for relaxing.

For the Abrams, the routine of finding ways to be together was a hallmark of family culture. There were many evenings when one or more of them had to be out of the house for a meeting or a sports event, or times when David or Sara had work phone calls they had to make in private. Yet unless there was a reason for them to be apart, their natural tendency was to spend time together.

To be clear, the difference between the Steins and the Abrams is quite subtle. Both families spend quality time together, have family meals and joint activities. The distinction, as with most questions of culture, is almost imperceptible at times. But it is real and it has ramifications.

As children mature, parents in families that spend more of their down-time together will have a better awareness of their children's schoolwork and, more importantly, their social activities. Just think about the difference between a family where the child's computer or phone screen is naturally visible to the parents and a scenario where the parents see that screen only if they make a specific visit to check in on the child who is working alone in another room.

The children's behavior too will be affected by these distinctions. Paralleling our family scenario, researchers have found that children from different cultural backgrounds react differently to typical school situations. For example, children raised in individualistic cultures prefer working independently and see getting help from others as cheating, whereas those who come from a collectivist culture are more comfortable working with peers on collaborative projects and sharing credit or blame.[2]

HARNESSING THE POWER OF CULTURE

If subtle routines such as where we spend our time influence children's behavior, we can imagine the power that the full range of family culture has on their development. How can we harness this power?

---

2. See, for example, Michael S. Rosenberg, David Westling, and James McLeskey, *Special Education for Today's Teachers: An Introduction* (New York: Pearson, 2008), 63–64. See also David Leake and Rhonda Black, *Essential Tools: Improving Secondary Education and Transition for Youth with Disabilities. Cultural and Linguistic Diversity: Implications for Transition Personnel* (Minneapolis: ICI Publications Office, 2005), http://www.ncset.org/publications/essentialtools/diversity/EssentialTools_Diversity.pdf (accessed October 19, 2015).

Here we may be most successful if we take a cue from a different sphere: organizational psychology. For several decades, organizational psychologists have devoted significant effort to studying culture formation and change in businesses and organizations. Unlike a family, an organization is intentionally formed to serve particular functions. As a result, it is easier to see how its culture is proactively formed and guided.

Lee Bolman and Terrence Deal, two leading researchers in organizational theory, suggest that organizations can be viewed through four fundamental frames: structural, human resource, political, and symbolic.[3] As their names suggest, the first three of these frames are most appropriate for a business setting. Most parents do not employ a human resources manager – though at times they might wish they did.

The fourth frame, however, focuses on how cultural meaning is formed through symbolic elements like rituals, stories, metaphors, and heroes. If you want to understand how the symbolic frame works, there is nowhere better to look than your local army. Armies are faced with an unenviable challenge. They must take a group of young men and women, whether volunteers or conscripts, and in a span of months transform them into disciplined soldiers who are dedicated to following their commanders' orders even at the risk of grave personal danger.

While providing effective technical and physical training may be a challenge, the most difficult transition of basic training is engendering an emotional commitment in new recruits. To this end, armies enlist the full range of symbolic tools.

Recruits are given uniform clothing, haircuts, and standard-issue equipment as a symbol of belonging and unity. Basic training

---

3. Lee Bolman and Terrence Deal, *Reframing Organizations*, 5th ed. (New York: Jossey Bass, 2013).

is filled with rituals, from the first-day physical endurance test to daily roll call, group calisthenics, and the typical culminating hike and induction ceremony. In classroom sessions, recruits learn the stories of their predecessors' heroics in past army conquests. Rather than a salary bonus, individual achievements are recognized through symbolic rewards such as medals or promotion to a higher rank. The army's hierarchy is solidified through rituals like standing at attention or saluting a superior officer.

As the list extends well beyond these typical examples, we can easily see the influence of these symbolic acts in shaping the army's culture and the individual soldier's behavior. Most parents do not want their children to stand at attention and salute when they enter the room. But we do want to shape our family's culture. Both the army and Bolman and Deal's symbolic frame point us to powerful ways of doing so.

RITUALS

As committed Jews, we are quite familiar with rituals. We rarely go a day, or even an hour, without one. But when it comes to culture-setting in our families, these rituals are not necessarily sufficient.

Take the example of Havdala, the ritual that marks the conclusion of Shabbat. Each Saturday night Dan Stein comes home from synagogue with his son, Adam. Debbie and Rachel are waiting for them, eager to get moving with their evening plans. Dan quickly gathers the wine, spices, and candle as the family gathers around the kitchen counter. He recites Havdala and drinks the wine. The family answers "amen" and then everyone moves off on the way to their next activity.

Did the Steins fulfill the mitzva of Havdala? Absolutely. But a ritual conducted in this manner is certainly not something that will impact the family's culture in any meaningful way. For a different perspective, watch how Havdala unfolds in the Abram home.

As David returns home from synagogue, the Abram family starts to gather around the kitchen table. Their Havdala set consists of a spice box which Lisa made in kindergarten, a cup Jonny made in his camp's pottery activity, and a candle Ben purchased during his class trip to Israel. David doesn't have a particularly good voice, but the family always sings Havdala together. Afterwards they pause for a moment to wish one another a good week before transitioning back to their separate activities. Sometimes Sara asks each of the kids to share something they are looking forward to in the coming week before they go.

The Abrams have made Havdala into a weekly ritual that brings their family together, if just for a moment, reinforces their relationships, and imparts meaning to the week ahead. Ten minutes a week may not change their lives, but for the Abrams it certainly makes a difference.

MORE RITUALS

To be clear, not every mitzva must be a ritual. Sometimes Havdala can just be Havdala. But we should realize how many mitzvot have the potential to become this sort of family-strengthening and culture-setting ritual. For some families, it may be singing at the Shabbat table, for others it may be the way a specific holiday is celebrated, or the way they give *tzedaka* (charity) and host guests. The spectrum of mitzvot provides opportunities for us to create rituals that work for our particular family.

At the same time, it is important to realize that just as every mitzva need not be a ritual, not every ritual must be a mitzva. We have already seen some of the challenges that the Abrams encountered when their oldest son, Ben, turned twelve. His disorganization at school led to frustrations at home and created more tension than the family was used to. We have also seen how David and Sara worked to help Ben through that challenging stage.

What we have not yet addressed, however, is the underlying culture that helped David and Sara's efforts succeed. Beyond Havdala, the Abrams had naturally established a series of ongoing family rituals. From the time the Abram children were young, they looked forward to family movie night. Each week on Saturday or Sunday evening, David would make the popcorn, Sara and the kids would choose the film, and the family would stay up late watching together. In the summer time, the movie might be replaced by a s'mores cookout or a picnic, but one way or another everyone knew that they would be spending that time together.

A number of more subtle rituals also filled out the Abram family's week. Thursday night, for example, was always pizza night. Whether they had a special love for pizza or not, the consistency lent a rhythm and stability to the week. And while mornings were always a bit rushed, the kids all knew that before they ran out to the bus they would file past their mom. Instead of just a regular goodbye, Sara would give each of them a kiss and tell them they were going to "rock the day." A silly saying, perhaps, but it sent the Abram children off to school with a little more confidence, feeling loved and connected to a special and unique family. This culture of connectedness was crucial in helping the Abrams get through challenging times with Ben or any of their children.

STORIES

Let's turn back for a moment to Viktor Frankl. We focused earlier on Frankl's inspirational notion that our most precious freedom is the ability to choose how we wish to respond to the stimuli around us. But Frankl's theory of human behavior extends well beyond this key concept. Frankl titled his seminal work, *Man's Search for Meaning*. The title encapsulates the true core of human behavior according to Frankl. Simply put, the most elevating and satisfying of all human endeavors is to create meaning in the world around us.[4]

And how do we create meaning? We tell stories.

Since the beginning of humanity, people have told stories. The ancients told stories about how the moon was made or how unusual animals came to be. Stories of good people and their reward, and of the evil and their punishment.

Modern people tell stories as well. We do not talk as much about how the beaver got its tail or why the camel has its hump, but we do tell our own stories to explain the world around us. These narratives form the backbone of family culture and shape the way we and our children see the world. Some of them are actual stories, like this one, which Dan Stein liked to tell his children:

> Grandfather Hershel was the first member of the Stein family to arrive in America. He came here as a fourteen-year-old boy. Like many Jewish immigrants, he came through Ellis Island with nothing to his name. Hershel was taken in by cousins in a small Lower East Side tenement. The cousins could not afford to feed an extra mouth, so Hershel tried to provide for himself by peddling second-hand clothing on the street corners. He struggled for years, not knowing if he would have enough to eat the next day.
>
> Shortly after he married, Hershel developed more of a sense for business. With a few shrewd deals, he was able to earn enough to open his own clothing store. It was then that the Stein family finally came to be secure and established in

---

4. Both Jerome Bruner and Lev Vygotsky, in their works referenced in Chapter 2, believe that meaning is socially constructed. In other words, the way we interpret the world around us is inextricably linked to the context in which we live and the people with whom we interact.

America. With a steady income to rely on, they no longer had to scrounge for bargains or take hand-me-downs from relatives. For the first time since he had arrived in America, Hershel was happy.

All the Stein children and grandchildren knew Hershel's story. More important than the facts of the story were the values it emphasized, and the family culture it shaped. Some of these values, like hard work and dedication to family, had a positive impact on the children's development. Yet the central facet of the story, the link between money and happiness, had a lasting impact as well.

SHORTER STORIES

This brings us to the second kind of storytelling. These stories are not coherent comprehensive narratives like the tale of Hershel's immigration. Rather, they consist of a body of seemingly unimportant comments, quips, or observations through which we express our understanding and interpretation of the world around us. Taken together, these comments make up the narrative that we weave around our own lives, and they impact immeasurably the meaning we pass on to our children.

As is the case in many families, for the Steins these two types of storytelling were logically intertwined. If the dinner table conversation centered around a neighborhood family that seemed discontented, Dan's first question typically centered around their financial well-being. His inquiry was well-meaning, and he wanted to help, but the comment revealed what Dan saw as the fulcrum of personal happiness. So too when Adam was considering preliminary options for college. Dan would often encourage him to examine the college's career-placement services and the average salaries of alumni.

The combination of the Hershel tale and Dan's intermittent comments formed a significant part of the Stein family story. This narrative lent a particular meaning to the events in their own lives and those around them. More importantly, the cultural understanding and unconscious attitude that Dan's stories created will influence how financial considerations factor into his children's vital life-decisions.

BUILDING CONNECTIONS

There is another sort of meaning that our stories can create.

David Abram was never one to let a good story go to waste. His children knew that once he had started one of his favorites, there was no stopping him. And there was no story that David liked better than that of his friend Avi.

Avi and David had been best friends through college and law school. In many ways they were quite similar. They were both political science majors who loved to discuss current issues, and they both considered themselves activists. If there was a crisis in the world, they were the first on the street to demonstrate. If the free legal clinic needed an extra hand, they were the first to volunteer. As they prepared to graduate, though, they took different paths.

David felt compelled to follow the more traditional route. He took a summer internship followed by a job at a large firm. When the family moved out to the suburbs, David became a partner in a mid-size office close to their home.

Avi, however, felt a different calling as he prepared for graduation. His first job took him to Africa, where he lived in makeshift housing and gave legal assistance to impoverished refugees. As Avi settled down, he began working as the director of an Israel advocacy group, and later founded his own nonprofit designed to eliminate the U.S.-based funding sources of terrorist organizations.

Whenever David told this story, his children could hear the admiration in his voice. David always concluded the story in the same way: "You know, there are times in life when you hear that calling. It's just like the Torah says when God whispered to Avraham, '*lekh lekha* – start your journey.' We're still part of that same journey. There are times when God calls us to do something. And when that happens, we have to be ready."

JEWISH STORIES

Like Dan's anecdotes, the story that David tells shapes his family's culture. His stories become the family's stories. The values inherent in his narrative, such as social activism and service to others, are clear. But what is most striking is how David concludes the story. He moves seamlessly from a story about his friend to the biblical story of Avraham. By doing so David bridges the gap of generations.

Just as Avi's story becomes a personalized part of the Abram family culture, so too the tale of Avraham is woven into the family narrative. In the Abram family, rising to meet a challenge and pursuing one's mission in life is not just a value in and of itself, it is fulfillment of our responsibility as children of Avraham. This connection engenders a deeper commitment to the Abrams' values. Yet its true import extends well beyond the values themselves. David's narrative creates a link between his family's story and the story of the Jewish people. As a result, the Abrams interpret their lives and give meaning to their choices within the framework of Jewish history. Piece by piece, their family's personal narrative is intertwined with the story of the Jewish people.

Storytelling is itself a concept deeply embedded within Jewish tradition. As early as the events in the Book of Deuteronomy, on the eve of their entry into the Land of Israel, Moses instructs the people in the procedure of bringing the first fruits of the harvest season to the Temple. The farmer must not only bring his fruits to the priest. As he does so, he is instructed to retell the story of the Jewish people from their descent to Egypt through their redemption and ultimately their arrival in Israel. The farmer tells this story not as a series of historical events, however, but as a personal story. *"Arami oved avi...My father was a wandering Aramean."*[5]

The inclusion of a personal story as part of the Temple ritual is certainly unique. Later, the rabbis of the Mishna pick up on this story and mandate its exposition as the center of the Passover Seder. In doing so, they give the ancient story a life outside the Temple service and integrate it into the holiday of Passover, whose central feature is the transmission of the Jewish story from one generation to the next.

UPS AND DOWNS

Culture is fundamentally built through the mundane interactions of the daily routine. Yet the more pronounced highs and lows of life allow us to add vital layers of meaning. Here again we turn back to Viktor Frankl. As we saw earlier, Frankl's understanding of the human condition emerged from his horrific experiences during the Holocaust. No one should ever have to suffer the depravity which Frankl witnessed. Yet Frankl's work shows us how we can extract meaning from the relative lows in our lives.

How do we parent in challenging times?

David Abram had a number of good years at his law firm. But back when Ben was poised to enter high school and Jonny was about to start middle school, business started to dry up. The firm started to downsize, and David was told that his job would be among those cut before the end of the year.

---

5. Deuteronomy 26:5.

David began pounding the pavement immediately. After a few months of searching, it became clear that local opportunities were very limited. The only way David could find another position was by agreeing to relocate.

Ben and Jonny had been looking forward to their new schools for months. They were devastated when David and Sara shared the news. The following few days at home were rough, to put it mildly. The wrong word or look could send either boy into tears. Both Ben and Jonny spent many hours shut up in their room sulking. The Abrams had never seen their children like this, and they were scared. On top of that, David felt guilty that his professional struggles were spilling over onto his children.

After a few failed attempts to talk to the boys, David and Sara were out of ideas. Finally, Sara suggested they go back to the family motto: "When all else fails, eat ice cream." They piled the kids into the car and headed to the store. With their favorite flavors at hand, the Abrams sat down together on the grass outside. Sara turned to the boys and said, "This is tough on all of us. But we're a family. That means we will take care of each other and figure out how to get through this together. No matter how much ice cream it takes!"

That one outing did not resolve all the challenges. Ben and Jonny still had to work through leaving their friends, adjusting to a new school and community. However, Sara succeeded in reframing how they interpreted the challenges. She helped Ben and Jonny understand that while they could not control the events that affected them, they could control how they reacted to the events. Sara underscored that the Abram family responds to challenges by coming together. By doing so, she helped the children come to terms with the move and built an important piece of their family culture.

As they continue along their journey as a family, the Abrams may well face more challenging downturns than this. Sickness or the untimely passing of a loved one can shake a family to its core. No one can prescribe how a family must respond to such tragedies. However, here too Jewish tradition gives us guidance. The process of sitting shiva, for example, leads families that have suffered a loss to spend a week mourning together. That week is a crucial time for family members to help one another find comfort and extract a sense of meaning from tragedy.

The relative high points in our lives provide a similar opportunity to shape our family culture. The stress of challenging times helps us realize that we must respond. It can be all too easy to miss the opportunities provided by the high points. If we are conscious of the potential offered us at these times, a bar or bat mitzva can be not only a family celebration but also a celebration of the family's values. If we understand the power of these emotional events, a triumph on the sports field can reinforce a culture of humility, and success in the academic arena can strengthen a sense of gratitude.

Admittedly, the concept of culture seems somewhat abstract. To remind ourselves of its concrete importance, however, we have only to refer back to the "rules" of the Abram family. Through a combination of rituals, storytelling, and making meaning out of both ordinary and highly charged emotional events, the Abrams have created a family culture where values, ideals, and relationships simply become part-and-parcel of how each member of the family functions each day.

Chapter Ten

Teenagers ...

All of this logical, rational thought about parenting is wonderful. But put it up against a typical teenager, and Sunday afternoons start to go something like this:

Adam is halfway out the front door as he calls, "Mom, I'm taking the car to go out with my friends. I'll be home later." He knows very well that he needs to get permission to take his mom's car. Dan and Debbie have to know where he is headed, and Debbie certainly has a right to know when Adam will return with *her* car. This is not the first time Adam has tried a quick exit, and Debbie is not about to let him get away with it again. The conversation quickly boils over:

> *Debbie:* Wait a second. You know you can't just leave without telling me where you are going or who you are going with. Besides, your father needs your help around the house today.
> *Adam:* That's ridiculous. I'm sixteen years old and I have the right to do what I want on a Sunday. None of my friends have to stay home to help their parents.

> *Debbie:* Now you're being rude. You are planning to take my car. What if I need it? You didn't even bother telling me when you're coming home.
>
> *Adam:* Fine. Forget it. You can keep your car, but I'm going out.

With a slam of the door Adam is walking to a friend's home and Debbie is left fuming. She wonders whether she should have tried harder to stop him. More than that, Debbie wonders what she did to deserve this. These fights are happening almost daily, and Debbie does not know how she will get through the next two years of living with an angry teenager. Adam is only in tenth grade and high school graduation seems very far away.

Debbie is certainly not alone in her struggles. Across Western society, teenagers are notorious for driving their parents crazy from the time they hit puberty until the moment they leave for college. And it is easy to see why. Teens tend to have extreme emotions. They are more likely to engage in risk-taking behavior and ignore the potential consequences of their actions. On top of that, teens are more likely to rebel against authority figures, defy parental guidance, and distance themselves from their families.

UNDERSTANDING TEEN BEHAVIOR

So how are we to survive our children's adolescence?

Our best shot is to go back to what we started with: putting our children at the center. Given the amount of emotional energy that teenagers demand of us, it often seems that they are already at center stage in our family drama. Yet the ironic truth is that the more our teens act out, the less likely we are to place them at the center in a healthy way.

When our younger children misbehave, we may be frustrated with them. We may even become angry and confrontational.

Yet the younger the child is, the more likely we are to come back to understanding her behavior from Glasser's choice theory perspective.[1]

We know intuitively that our five-year-old is not having a tantrum because she is out to get us. She is having a tantrum because she does not know how else to meet her needs. This recognition makes it easier to understand her needs from a developmental perspective, and allows us to help her work through the struggles of the moment.

But when it comes to our fifteen-year-old, all of this is more difficult for us to process. The fifteen-year-old looks more like an adult. He may be our height (or taller). He walks and talks and eats like an adult. And so we forget just how different it is to be a teenager, and we fall into the trap of interpreting our teen's actions through an adult lens.

If an adult slammed the door, cursed at us under his breath, or rolled his eyes as we attempted to speak to him we would be justified in our indignation. When our teens do all of this and more, it is natural to feel angry, but it is not helpful to act on those feelings. We will be much more successful if we are able to take a step back and remind ourselves that teens are definitely not adults. Rather, adolescents are in the middle of a journey through a fundamentally unique and challenging phase of their development.

BIOLOGICAL CHALLENGES

There are many biological factors at play in an adolescent. Some of these are linked directly to impulsive decision-making, risk-taking behavior, and limited ability to modulate emotions. Neurologists have shown through magnetic resonance brain imaging

---

1. We introduced and discussed William Glasser's choice theory as a foundation for our approach to discipline in Chapter 8.

that the key brain functions of judgment and self-control simply do not function as well during adolescence. Other researchers have shown that changes in brain hormone function, particularly dopamine receptors, produce a loss of emotional buffering capacity that is at the heart of adolescents' tendency to seek greater sensation rewards.

In case human teen behavior was not proof enough of all this, scientists have shown that adolescent mice exhibit lack of judgment in a classic teenage manner by drinking too much ethanol alcohol in controlled experiments. Even more striking, adolescent male mice drink significantly more when they drink in groups![2]

On their own, any one of these findings could be questioned. But what we have just listed here is a small sample. Taken as a whole, the research on teenage development makes it clear that there are direct, physically identifiable factors underlying typical adolescent behavior. For our purposes, the details of neurons, hormones, and brain cortexes are not crucial. What is essential is that we realize that our teen's inability to avoid poor judgments

---

2. For some of the research on teenage risk-taking, both in humans and in mice, see http://www.sciencedaily.com/releases/2007/04/070412115231.htm (accessed September 11, 2015) and http://www.newyorker.com/magazine/2015/08/31/the-terrible-teens (August 30, 2015).

  Also see Laurence Steinberg's comprehensive article, "A Social Neuroscience Perspective on Adolescent Risk-Taking," http://www.ncbi.nlm.nih.gov/pmc/articles/PMC2396566/ (accessed September 11, 2015). Steinberg posits thoughtful questions on the causes of adolescent risk-taking behavior. For our purposes, however, the precise scientific cause is less material than the fundamental understanding that certain biological and neurological factors distinguish adolescence from the other stages of development. This reality reminds us that no matter how much teens look like adults, they must be treated in a different, developmentally appropriate manner. For a more practical application, see Frances E. Jensen, *The Teenage Brain: A Neuroscientist's Guide to Raising Adolescents and Young Adults* (New York: HarperCollins, 2015).

is as natural as our five-year-old's inability to pour the milk without spilling. Yelling, scolding, or punishing will not help the five-year-old's hands grow stronger. In just the same way, no amount of reprimanding can enable fifteen-year-old synapses to function more effectively.

As leading researchers have noted, the physical realities of adolescence are the fundamental reason behind the failure of all public health initiatives to effectively curb teens' risk-taking behavior.[3] Within our own families, accepting these realities is the first key to understanding the developmental stage of adolescence. It allows us to recognize that teen behavior that seems malicious is actually just the next (and more challenging) step in our children's natural development. With this knowledge in mind, we are better poised to navigate ourselves through the natural frustrations of living with a teenager. And we must find our own emotional balance before we can respond successfully to the challenges posed by our teens.

THE SEARCH FOR IDENTITY

And yet, for teenagers, biology is only half the story. The other half of what adolescents are going through, and what they put their parents through, is a complex psychological phenomenon best described by the psychoanalyst Erik Erikson. Erikson's work focused on the development of personality over the course of an individual's lifetime. His perspective is particularly helpful because he focuses on the individual's development in relation to the individual's social surroundings.

Although Erikson's stages reach from birth all the way to older adulthood, he underscores the crucial importance of the personal development that takes place during adolescence.

---

3. See Steinberg's article referenced in the preceding note.

As Erikson explains, during puberty, teenagers become more conscious of how others perceive them, including the expectations of peers and parents. Their awareness of the perceptions held by others often conflicts with their own self-image, thereby causing identity and role confusion. This is the crux of the conflict inherent in the teenage years. As a result, the most crucial task of adolescence is to negotiate what Erikson terms the "identity crisis."

What does a classic identity crisis look like?

Ben Abram has always been a well-behaved kid. He was the child who always helped his mom before being asked, the first-born son who wanted to please parents and teachers alike. This attitude carried over to his religious observance. Ben was a super-star at his bar mitzva. He read from the Torah, led the prayers, and delivered a wonderful speech. Following his bar mitzva, Ben willingly went to synagogue with his father every Shabbat, much to David's delight.

At the beginning of tenth grade, however, things began to change. At first Ben just seemed more sullen and moved more slowly when it came time to go to synagogue on Saturday mornings. Then he began to push back more directly, saying he preferred to pray at home instead. As the weeks went on, it became clear to the Abrams that Ben actually was not doing much praying at home, not even little things like making blessings before and after eating.

One of Ben's teachers mentioned that Ben was no longer volunteering to lead prayers at school and that it was a challenge to even get him into the room each time. More than that, the teacher reported, Ben now seemed disengaged in the Judaic classes where he used to shine. Lately, if Ben did speak up in class, it was only to ask to go to the bathroom or to crack a cynical remark.

All of this was extremely difficult for David and Sara to watch. Ben's Jewish education and his love of Jewish tradition and prayer were at the center of what they wanted for his life. They were frustrated with Ben's behavior. They did not know what it meant, and they certainly did not know what to do about it. Above all, they were concerned about Ben's Jewish future.

HOW TO RESPOND

Ben's behavior is a teenage challenge that has nothing to do with poor judgment or impulsive behavior. Rather, Ben is navigating an identity crisis. As a child and pre-teen, Ben accepted his role without question. That is not to say he never misbehaved, but when he came late to prayers at a younger age, it was because he was distracted by a friend or lost track of time. Fundamentally, Ben thought of himself – like his father – as an individual committed to prayer, Jewish learning, and Jewish observance.

But moving through adolescence Ben began to more deeply examine the roles he had previously accepted. The identity which came from others began to seem like an external, sometimes ill-fitting, mask. Ben found himself subconsciously pushing against that identity as he began to search for one that felt more his own. This is an entirely natural process. Yet it is painful for parents to watch.

So how should the Abrams respond to Ben's pushback?

To have any chance of success, David and Sara must understand what lies behind Ben's behavior. Ben is pushing back against an identity that he feels has come from others. It would be easy for the Abrams to stumble now because they misunderstand what is behind this pushback.

David and Sara have worked for years to cultivate Ben's values and commitments. They have been very purposeful in helping him to create this identity. When Ben pushes back against this identity, they cannot help but feel that he is pushing them, and their values, away.

TWO PITFALLS

This natural feeling typically leads to two parental reactions. First, we want to redouble our efforts to enforce the very ideals that our teen seems to be deserting. Sara and David do not want to see Ben distance himself from participating in prayer. And so they may raise the stakes through rewards, punishment, or whatever form of coercion seems necessary to force him to participate. This direct, forceful approach allows us to feel a sense of control. More than that, if we force our teen to act as if nothing has changed, we can allay our own fears by pretending all is as it once was.

Second, as we watch our teen rebuff the identity we gave him, we are likely to feel personally rejected. The Abrams feel that Ben is not only distancing himself from their commitments, he is distancing himself from them. To protect themselves, David and Sara will be tempted to create emotional distance on the parental side of the relationship. They will want to shrug off Ben's scowls and brush past his resistance so that it does not sting quite as much.

These two reactions reinforce each another. The more emotional distance we create, the easier it is to hammer our teen into compliance. And each time we hammer, we widen the chasm dividing parent and child. Both of these parental reactions are natural survival mechanisms. But an effective approach to raising adolescents takes just the opposite approach.

A BALANCED APPROACH

Fortunately, David and Sara do not give in to either of these temptations. At first, David wants to force Ben to join him at shul, and he tries that for a few weeks. But seeing that Ben continues to protest, David changes his tune. He has always believed that parenting is not about what happens today, it's about what happens down the road. Pushing Ben too hard now may backfire as Ben starts making his own adult decisions all too soon.

This doesn't mean that David suddenly has all the answers. Each Saturday morning David goes through a debate with himself: Should he force Ben to come to synagogue or let him stay home? If Ben stays home, does he still need to wake up on time? Does he need to pray on his own? For how long? If Ben does come to synagogue, David wonders how many times he should tap Ben on the shoulder or make sure he is on the right page.

As the weeks go by, David continues to navigate through this tension. He gives his son some leeway to make decisions but still demands that Ben meet the basic expectations of family life. David often feels like he is holding a butterfly in cupped hands. Close too tightly and the insect will be crushed, open too wide and it will fly away.

Most important, David talks to Ben throughout this process. This is more challenging than it may seem. Take this exchange, for example:

> *David:* OK, Ben. It's time for us to get going to shul. You didn't come last week and you promised you would join me this week.
>
> *Ben:* Do I really have to? Why are you making me?

At this point, faced with Ben's heavy sigh and roll of the eyes, David wants to respond by saying, "You have to come because I said so! Now stop giving me a hard time and let's go!"

Instead, David takes a deep breath and says: "I know you don't want to do this right now. But this is what our family believes in. Shul is a very significant part of my life, and davening consistently has helped me get through some rough times over the years. I think it's made me a better person as a result. I don't make you come every time, but I also don't want you to drop it entirely before you know what you are missing."

Living in the constant push-pull of this middle ground is difficult for parents, and openly explaining our beliefs to sarcastic adolescents is even more challenging. Yet this is exactly what our teens need. As Erikson explains, adolescents are engaged in a search for their own identities. This search includes questioning parent-given identities and trying out alternative identities. Compelling compliance can short-circuit this search process and leave the adolescent in what Erikson calls "identity confusion." Such identity confusion can lead to various levels of difficulty in forming relationships, developing commitments, and building a healthy adult life. If we want our children to become well-adjusted adults, we must allow them to build their own identities when they are teens.

THE OTHER DIRECTION?

But there is another way to resolve the tension. Adolescents require autonomy in order to develop their personal identities. Why not just give them full freedom to make their own decisions? David will certainly have an easier time each Saturday morning if he just lets Ben make his own choice about prayers, and Ben will be fully enabled to create his own self-determination.

We need only turn back to teen impulse control and judgment issues to see how wrong things can go if we let adolescents make decisions without parental boundaries. Debbie Stein won't let sixteen-year-old Adam take the car without telling her where he is going. Imagine what would happen if she does not stop him, and his ill-conceived plans include piling too many friends in the car, staying out too late, or otherwise increasing the likelihood that he will not make it home safely. And that is to say nothing of scenarios where drugs, alcohol, or other high-risk activities might be involved. Clearly, for safety's sake, there need to be parental boundaries.

In Ben's case, however, it is unlikely that anything dangerous will result from oversleeping. And very few people have been directly injured from a lack of prayer. Yet here, too, David will be doing Ben a disservice if he gives him a free pass on his obligations. This is the other side of the identity crisis.

We cannot stymie our teens' search for their own identities, but neither can we absent ourselves from the search process. Adolescents question the identities given them by their parents. At the same time, they work to reconstruct their own identities as they navigate through the multiple spheres that now demand their attention. James Fowler, whose work on faith development we saw earlier, identifies adolescence with Stage 3 synthetic-conventional faith. In this stage, "faith must provide a coherent orientation in the midst of…[a] more complex and diverse range of involvements."[4] In other words, adolescents are constructing their own identities partly by synthesizing and responding to the ideas and commitments which surround them.

VALUES IN VIEW

We want our values to be part of the landscape that our teenagers synthesize during their identity development. This can happen only if those values are a clear and present part of our children's lives. If David never forces Ben to join him in synagogue, the synagogue experience will not be part of Ben's developmental process. If David never demands that Ben pray, Ben will not be positioned to incorporate this spiritual process into his identity formation.

Moreover, we know that adolescents are particularly attuned to what they perceive as hypocrisy. While Ben might be happy to sleep in, on some level he will see his father's leniency as inconsistency. Ben may resist when David pushes him to come to

---

4. James W. Fowler, *Stages of Faith* (New York: Harper & Row, 1981).

synagogue; but at the same time, he will note his father's commitment to the practice of this value. That commitment again becomes part of the landscape that helps to shape Ben's development.

This balanced approach allows Ben to explore while ensuring that his journey is filled with the Abram family's ideals. Yet it will be of little use if the Abrams fall into the second emotional trap and distance themselves from Ben to avoid the pain of his rejection. By the time our children hit adolescence, we have poured years of emotional effort and energy into their education and development. Seeing them rebuff some of that education is naturally frustrating.

Here is where we most misunderstand our teens. David and Sara see that Ben is questioning what they have taught him. Their logical conclusion is that Ben is dissatisfied with them or disillusioned with their ideals. Either option feels like a personal rejection. But Erikson's identity crisis teaches us that Ben is not rebuffing his parents because of who they are. Nor is he renouncing what their ideals represent.

As he enters adolescence, Ben develops the ability to craft his own self-made identity. This makes any externally derived identity feel suspect. Ben questions his childhood identity simply because it is not one of his own creation. The process of questioning, testing, and exploring is the only way that Ben can make any identity, however similar or different, into his own. Understanding this does not do away with David and Sara's pain entirely, but it tempers the frustration sufficiently for them to take a different emotional approach.

STAYING TOGETHER

After one particularly frustrating Saturday afternoon, David and Sara are up late talking about how to handle Ben. The following day will be one of the few Sundays when there are no soccer games, youth groups, or major chores scheduled. It seems like a great day for a family outing. But with the attitude that Ben has been displaying recently, they are not sure. If they leave Ben to his own devices, he will make plans to go out with his friends, leaving David and Sara to a much more peaceful afternoon with the other children.

> *Sara:* Why don't we just let Ben do his own thing tomorrow? He doesn't want to be with us most days anyway.
> *David:* It would definitely be easier. That way we won't have to deal with the eye-rolling when we tell the kids our plans for the day. But it doesn't feel right to just let him check out like that.
> *Sara:* I know he's going through a lot now. It would probably do us all some good to spend the time together.

Sara realizes that this is about what *Ben* is going through and not a rejection of her or her values. This realization allows her to avoid the temptation to distance herself from her son. Instead Sara musters the courage to open the door to reinforcing the parent-child connection. This Sunday the reinforcement will come through a family outing. Another time Sara might convince Ben to join her as she runs errands or David might take Ben out for some extra practice as he gets ready for his driving test. Ben will not always be pleasant – even when they are doing things that are for his own benefit. Yet Sara and David are committed to maintaining their emotional connection to their teen.

THE NEED FOR RELATIONSHIP

Why are the Abrams' efforts so important? The same lesson that Fowler taught us about values in Chapter 5 is relevant for relationships as well. Just as our ideals are part of the landscape that shapes our children's development, our relationships with them must also be part of their growth process. Overbearing parents may cause their teens to rebel, but emotionally distant parents can offer no guidance at all.

Everything we learned about the importance of relationships is true for adolescents as well. It is just more of a challenge to implement. In fact, thinking about what is to come in the teenage years is perhaps the best reminder of how important it is for us to forge strong relationships when our children are still young. Our five- and ten-year-olds need us in ways that sometimes seem like a burden. Yet those needs give us opportunities to build the kinds of relationships that will stand the test of the turbulent teens.

William Glasser's theory further highlights the necessity for this emotional connection. Glasser explains that what we see as discipline problems are typically just instances of normal kids trying to meet their own physical, psychological, or emotional needs. As we learned earlier, emotions – and with them emotional needs – are more intense in adolescence than at any other time. Though parents will not be able to meet all of their teens' emotional needs, strengthening their relationship with the teen will maximize the emotional support they can offer – and minimize the kids' need to meet their needs in other ways.

PEER GROUPS

While we want to maximize our support for our children, we also must be realistic. Research shows that, as children enter adolescence, there is a drastic increase in the impact of peer influence on their behavioral choices.[5] Nowhere is this phenomenon more obvious than in your local high school.

---

5. See, for example, Darcy Santor, Deanna Messervey, and Vivek Kusumaka, "Measuring Peer Pressure, Popularity, and Conformity in Adolescent Boys and Girls: Predicting School Performance, Sexual Attitudes, and Substance Abuse," *Journal of Youth and Adolescence* 29, no. 2 (2000): 163–82.

Consider the following scenario: In one locality, the high school had a dress code. The students would typically arrive each morning dressed in uniform and complaining about the lack of freedom it implied. In an attempt to give them the freedom to express their individuality, the principal did away with the dress code for a day. The results were striking.

As he waited to greet the students on "dress-down day," the principal was shocked to see that one student after the next arrived in the identical jeans and T-shirt ensemble that was the current fashion.[6] Rather than expressing their individuality, the students had simply traded one uniform for another. As the principal saw firsthand, while adolescents rebel against adult authority, they are more than happy to submit to the authority of their peers.

This is not just about what you might think of as peer pressure. These students were not encouraged by their friends to wear jeans and T-shirts, just as our teens are not facing any overt pressure to conform to the latest hairstyles, music, or digital entertainment preferences. To be sure, there are times when teens are pushed by their friends to make specific choices. The phenomenon, however, is much broader than those instances.

As children enter adolescence, they gain an intense awareness of their social environment coupled with a strong desire to fit in with it.[7] Ultimately this will serve our children well, enabling them to integrate into adult society. Social awareness is what ensures that we speak, act, and dress in ways that other adults deem appropriate. But for adolescents the same awareness means

---

6. Judd Kruger Levingston relates this story from his personal experience as a principal in *Sowing the Seeds of Character: The Moral Education of Adolescents in Public and Private Schools* (Westport, Conn.: Praeger, 2009).

7. Both Erikson and Fowler highlight these factors in their developmental theories.

that the desire to fit in with peers will influence their choices in a manner that we wish we could avoid.

There are certainly times when parents will need to push back against this sort of peer influence. Doing so, however, will almost always come at an emotional cost. Imagine that your teen attends the school described in our dress code story. What would it take for you to convince him to wear a button-down shirt on dress-down day? If our teenagers feel that "all their friends" are doing something, whether it is a late-night group outing, watching a certain movie, or dressing in accord with a fashion trend, preventing them from following suit will be an uphill battle.

When the time comes that we are faced with these battles, we will need to choose which we must fight and which we should let pass. Yet there may be an alternative. If we know that peer influence will be a major factor in our teenagers' lives, we may be able to proactively harness its power. How can we do so?

We have shared a number of examples from the life of the Abram family. But David and Sara were not the first "Abram-type" family in their community. When Ben was in lower school, David and Sara would often talk about other parents in the community who seemed to have one good kid after another. The Abrams started to look at what those older kids were involved with during their high school years and they began to notice some patterns.

Almost without exception, the teens who so impressed them were involved in the same activities. They worked in one of the youth groups, they gave of their time to a local social service agency, and they volunteered as big siblings for children with special needs. At first David and Sara assumed that these teenagers got involved *because* they were good kids. That was just part of the story, though. Over time the Abrams began to understand that the reverse was also true: these adolescents were acting like good kids *because* they were involved in organizations that surrounded them with a positive peer group.

David and Sara understood that if they wanted their own children to turn out like these kids, they needed frameworks that would expose their children to similarly positive peer influences. They also knew that once little Ben hit adolescence, he would not be looking to his parents to direct his extracurricular choices. So David and Sara worked in advance to create a path that would eventually lead Ben toward positive peer influences.

If any of the local youth groups had programs for lower-school children, David and Sara made sure Ben could attend. When the social service agency held a family volunteer day, the Abrams were there with their kids. They even chose their shul based on what teen activities it offered. And when it came time to select a middle school and high school for their children, the Abrams looked more at the student body than at the faculty.

This groundwork positioned the Abram children to find themselves naturally surrounded by a positive peer group by the time they reached adolescence. As a result, Sara and David succeeded in shifting the framework for the typical teenage struggles. In some peer groups, teens navigating the identity crisis would see risk-taking behaviors such as substance abuse as a natural outlet. In contrast, Ben might scowl in the morning or give his parents a hard time about going to shul, but they could take comfort in knowing that his peer group naturally positioned him to seek much more benign outlets for his adolescent struggles.

Even with all of this in mind, we must acknowledge that despite the best preparation and most level-headed parenting, there are no guarantees or simple solutions when it comes to teenagers. Here is where we have to take comfort in the final word on adolescence. While the teenage years may seem interminable, they do eventually pass. In fact, every adult we know has made it through this period one way or another. Bearing in mind that "this too shall pass" can help us keep our kids at the center and maintain our relationships with them as we navigate through the roller coaster of adolescence.

Conclusion

No matter how much we have learned about parenting, each of us has days when we feel more like the Steins than the Abrams. We wake up late and find ourselves yelling at our children as we rush out the door. Or we come home from a long day at work and our children manage to push exactly the button that makes us snap. Sometimes it's just the fact that we rarely get a vacation from parenting. It is natural to feel worn down on occasion.

We have to realize that the Abrams also have their bad days. Every parent does. So what ultimately distinguishes the Steins from the Abrams?

Fundamentally, it comes down to perspective. As we learned in Chapter 1, effective parenting begins by putting our children at the center. More than just the amount of time and attention we devote to our children, putting kids at the center means challenging ourselves to see things from their perspective rather than our own.

The tricky thing about perspective is that it can shift fairly easily. Fresh off a cup of coffee on a Sunday morning, we may be quite successful in seeing our toddler's desire to pour herself milk from her perspective. Flip the scenario to dinner at the end of a work day and it may suddenly become more difficult for us to understand her request as anything more than an annoyance.

In truth, the best way to understand perspective is to view it like a rubber band. Our most natural tendency is to see the world, and our children, from our own vantage point. Yet we must develop the ability to stretch ourselves to look at things from another angle, to see the world from the perspective of others. Because taking our children's viewpoint is indeed a stretch, we will inevitably slip back into our own perspective over time. There is no way to prevent this. The only solution is to "re-stretch."

How do we re-stretch?

Parenting is something that we do every day of the week. Because it is such a ubiquitous part of our lives, the parenting habits we develop and the manner in which we become used to relating to our children fade seamlessly into our subconscious. The first step in elevating these habits is to become aware of them, to begin to consciously consider how we relate to our kids.

In fact, perhaps the most important contribution made by the theories and approaches we have shared in these chapters is that they cause us to reflect on our approach to parenting. The details of the strategies we have presented may work perfectly for some families, but require adjustment or recalibrating to be helpful for others. Putting children at the center means that each parent must evaluate any given strategy not as a general concept but on the basis of its success when applied to a particular child. In the final analysis, if these approaches have caused us to think carefully about how we parent, and if they have caused us to reflect, to question and to stretch ourselves as we relate to our children, then they have accomplished the most crucial of tasks.

We conclude with the understanding that putting our children at the center also means recognizing that they are fundamentally independent individuals – different and distinct from our own identities. As much as we might like to, we cannot direct or control them. Our role is to extend ourselves in order to support and facilitate their growth. Effective parenting is as challenging as it is important, but if we can truly put our children at the center, our reward will be to watch as they lead amazing lives of their own creation.

The fonts used in this book are from the Arno family

Maggid Books
The best of contemporary Jewish thought from
Koren Publishers Jerusalem Ltd.